Death of a Purser

Hugh Richard Walter

McElroy

Chief Purser of the RMS Titanic

BIOGRAPHY

Frankie McElroy

Chief Purser Hugh McElroy in Purser's uniform, showing the ribbon for the Transport Medal with the South African clasp, in 1909

DEATH OF A PURSER

authorHOUSE®

AuthorHouse™
1663 Liberty Drive
Bloomington, IN 47403
www.authorhouse.com
Phone: 1-800-839-8640

First published by AuthorHouse   10/03/2011

ISBN: 978-1-4567-9042-4 (sc)
ISBN: 978-1-4567-9043-1 (ebk)

Printed in the United States of America

I would like to dedicated this research manuscript to my

Mum and Nan

I love and miss you both

I have kept my promise to both of you in doing this bioresearch
the world can now know the truth
with regards to Hugh
and hopefully have a better understanding

Slan agus beannacht De leat

(Good Health and God's blessing on you)

Forward

Purser Hugh McElroy is often mentioned in the literature about the Titanic and his photograph with Captain Smith on the deck of the Titanic is well known, but little was known about the man himself. Frankie McElroy has made it a lifelong quest to research the life of his great uncle Hugh, travelling extensively and meeting with family members, and this fascinating biography is the result.

Hugh was a great friend of my grandparents, a frequent visitor to their home whenever his ship was in Liverpool, and he was godfather to my father, Michael Gerard Hugh Worthy, born in Liverpool in February 1911 and named Hugh in his honour.

My grandfather, Michael J. Worthy, had much in common with Hugh, both being from staunch Catholic families with Irish ancestry and sharing a similar experience, in that my grandfather had been a Benedictine monk for several years before deciding, like Hugh, that the religious life was not for him.

It was a matter of deep regret to my father, still a baby at the time of Hugh's death, that he was never personally to know Hugh, who had been held in such high regard by the family.

Hugh has always remained, therefore, a heroic but shadowy figure and it is a delight to learn so much more of the man and his life from this biography, a valuable addition to the literature on the Titanic.

Veronica Jones

Michael Gerard Hugh Worthy and Nurse Morris

Contents

Chapter 1

The Family with life

The Dynasty of this family has at last been conveyed to paper and the research was carried out in two ways, firstly though a family genealogy contact and secondly through badgering and annoying my family for information, I would like to dedicate this bioresearch of my Great Uncle to the memory of my Mum and Nan, who I miss every day, "You will always be in my every thought".

I have decided to make my starting point with Richard Alfred McElroy, who was born in the year 1780 in West Derby, Liverpool, then In 1811 he married a lady named Elizabeth Anne, who was born in 1787 and was originally from Norfolk, in March 1814 she gave birth to twins, first a boy Richard, then a while later, she gave birth to another boy, Hugh, but because of massive complication she endured during childbirth with Hugh she died, at the age of just 27, which was a common event with complication in the early nineteenth century, due to lack of specialist obstetric care and doctors, Richard Alfred lived till he was 53 and died in 1833.

Richard Alfred's son Richard always held it against his brother Hugh, for his mother dying in childbirth, which is the reason behind the family "twin" graves, Richard did not want to be buried in the same grave as his brother, so after Richard's marriage to Mary in 1844 (who was from Fleetwood in Lancashire), he stipulated that his grave would only be for his wife, himself, and any family he may be blessed with, two years later, Mary gave birth to a boy, after a complicated childbirth, both mother and child survived, their son was christened William, at the age of 10, he was admitted into hospital, where they found he had contracted tubercle bacillus (tuberculosis), after a short stay in hospital, he died, and was buried in Richard's family plot, one of the family twin graves in Anfield Cemetery, Liverpool, Richard and Mary moved to West Derby after losing William, from that point, contact between the two family's was very spars.

In 1836, Richard Alfred's other son, Hugh, who lived at the family home, and was by then just 22 years old, had met a lovely Irish girl named Bridget, who was (we believe) from County Tipperary, Ireland. she was aged just 16, (she had emigrated to England with her parents when she was 9 years old) Hugh and Bridget fell in love immediately, and they married in August 1839, then in 1844, she gave birth firstly to a son, Richard Michael, two years later in the spring she gave birth to a daughter, Mary Hannah; Bridget had problems at birth with both children, it may be a coincidence, but both children died at the age of 44, Mary Hannah never got married and stayed with her mother, Mary Hannah herself died in 1890, her father Hugh, died in 1870.

The 1891 census it shows Bridget (Ireland), aged 70, living at 37a, Shaw Street, Everton, Liverpool (living on her own means). She had a 17 year old boarder, John Wilson, who worked as a clerk and was from Ireland (she possibly took in a boarder to help offset the bills) there were also two General Domestic, Mary Ellison who was from Liverpool aged 50, also Mary

MacCabe also from Liverpool, aged 27 years. Bridget died at home in Shaw Street, Liverpool, on the 8th November 1897, aged 77 years.

Richard Michael McElroy who was the son of Hugh and Bridget, was born 1844 in Liverpool, and in 1869 married Jessie Fox, who was born 1847 in Edinburgh, Scotland, Jessie was brought up by her father Michael Fox in St Cuthbert, Midlothian, Scotland, after her mother died in June 1867, Richard and Jessie, started their married life at 9, Cheshire Crescent, Great Crosby, Waterloo, Seaforth, Liverpool, in the 1871 Census shows Richard aged 25 and Jessie aged 23, they shared their home with Jessie's sister Charlotta Lucy Fox who was aged 29, she had moved from 14, Georges Square, St Cuthbert, Edinburgh, Midlothian after a request from Jessie, to come and stay, while they set up home, there was also a General Domestic, Ann Jane Corlett aged 28, who was from Castletown, on the Isle of Man.

In 1872 Richard and Jessie moved house to 3, Percy Street, Liverpool, which was a larger house, more in line for a family, along with this move Jessie's sister, Charlotta, returned back to Scotland, to look after her father, who had become very ill. Richard and Jessie were the driving force in this family being both staunch Roman Catholic and both coming from good middleclass backgrounds; their first child was born in Waterloo Hospital, Liverpool in June 1871 and they named her Charlotte Mary Louise, after Jessie's sister Charlotta, then in 1873 Jessie gave birth to a second girl Josephine Bridget, who was named after her Grandmother, (Bridget). Josephine was also born in Waterloo Hospital, Liverpool, because Jessie had complications with her at birth.

Richard and Jessie celebrated the birth of their first son, whom they named Hugh Richard Walter McElroy, he was born 28th October 1874 at 3, Percy Street, three years later Jessie gave birth to Hugh's younger brother Richard who was born in Waterloo Hospital, Liverpool in 1877 and christened Richard Marie Alphonsus McElroy, in those days (and also today) only the first born were born in hospital, unless there are complications, as there was with Josephine and Hugh's younger brother Richard.

In 1878 Hugh's two sisters, Charlotte aged 7 and Josephine aged 5, were enrolled to attend St Joseph's Convent, Gosford Green in Coventry as boarders for a convent education, the reason for enrolling them at St Joseph's Convent, was because of the very high standard of scholarship that was being attained there at that time, their mother Jessie also stayed in the convent residence, just to be near the girls, Jessie would return home as often as she could, to look after the boys, although Jessie was more at home in the convent, than the girls, because she also had a convent education and got on well with the Mother Superior and also the nuns, and, this arrangement was only until 1882, when the girls would finished their education, the convent had turned out girls, not only educated in the highest sense of the word but also with a truly religious background. St. Joseph's Convent was built in Raglan Street and was built of red brick with stone dressings, in the Early English style, the Convent Church which consisted of nave, apsidal chancel, side chapels, and baptistery ceased to be used after 1916, St. Joseph's Convent was destroyed by bombing during the Second World War, as was most of Coventry, but was survived by related foundations at Offchurch and Crackley Hall near Kenilworth.

In 1880, the family moved to 6, Eversley Street, Toxteth in Liverpool, then in 1882 at the age of 8, Hugh had passed through Preparatory School at St Mary's Lodge, St Leonards-on-Sea in Buckinghamshire, in 1885, Hugh went on to attended St Thomas College, which is part of

Cotton Hall Ecclesiastical College which is near Oakamoor in Staffordshire, as a boarder, along with his little brother Richard who also attended Cotton Hall at the same time, he too was a boarder, but he attended St Wilfrid's College which was part of their Preparatory School, they both remained in residence until 1888, when Hugh and Richard suddenly returned home, this was due to the death of their father, Hugh's brother Richard would return to Cotton Hall College, and stay until 1892 to finish his education, when at the age of 15 he would be employed in the accounts department as a clerk in the Liverpool Dock Board.

1881 Population Census, shows Richard and Jessie living at 6, Eversley Street, Toxteth, Liverpool, along with Hugh and his brother Richard also Rose Kingsley (34) Nurse/Domestic Servant. Charlotte and Josephine are not shown as they were attending St Joseph's Convent, Gosford Green in Coventry, but are shown on the 1881 Census for St Joseph's Convent.

While Hugh was attending Cotton College, he befriended another pupil Colin J. Cronin, who left at the same time as Hugh, they would both faithfully keep in contact right up to Colin untimely death at the young age of 24, Hugh on more than one occasion at Cotton Hall, according to the College news sheet "The Cottonian", though but a youngster, took part in the plays, with some success in the St Thomas College Theatre, even then gave evidence of a talent for portraying the humorous, which later in life, made him very popular as a ships officer with the White Star Line.

1891 Population census shows Richard aged 14, at Cotton College, with various other pupils between the ages of 12 to 17 years of age.

The family's next move was across the River Mersey to 6, Wilton Street, Liscard on the Wirral. Which was basically due to financial reasons after the death of Hugh's father, then suddenly on the 4th October 1899, Hugh's sister Josephine died of tubercle bacillus (tuberculosis), she was only aged 26, the church service was held in St Alban Roman Catholic Church in Mill Lane, Liscard (which was just around the corner from Wilton Street), and the burial, was at the family grave in Anfield Cemetery, in Liverpool, in those days there was no Mersey Roadway tunnel under the River Mersey, as we know it today, although proposals for crossing the River Mersey by road go back to at least 1825, but the actual construction of the road tunnel, started at end of 1925, and was finished on 18th July 1934.

That being so, Josephine's funeral had to go by the Liverpool Rail tunnel, which ran under the River Mersey linking Birkenhead and Liverpool, this tunnel was completed at the end of 1885. The trains were steam driven (they had a problem with the smoke which led to electrification in 1903), Josephine's funeral hearse was horse drawn, the funeral would take, quite some time, from St Alban Church in Liscard, to Birkenhead, her coffin would then go by steam train under the River Mersey, to be met on the Liverpool side at James Street Railway Station by another funeral hearse, then slowly on to the family grave in Anfield cemetery, in Liverpool, a journey that probably took about 6 or 7 hours, and today the same journey would take about 1 hour.

In the 1901 Census for 6, Wilton Street, it shows only Jessie (mother), Charlotte, Hugh and Richard and also a General Domestic, Rose Fox from Leitrim in Ireland.

After leaving Cotton College in 1888, Hugh then went on to attend St Francis College (Private) in Wimborne Minster, Dorsetshire, It is not therefore surprising given his upbringing that in

1890 when Hugh was aged just 16, and had just finished at St Francis College, he then decided to continue with his studies and become a student for the priesthood with the Canons Regular of the Lateran. At that time the Order's seminary was based at St Mary's Priory, in Bodmin, Cornwall. The Order's church was at St Mary's R.C. which is still there today, it is a lovely church complete with shrine to the right of the main door, Hugh first attended with the Canons Regular at St. Joseph's Priory, Marnhull Juniorate in Dorset where he took his Simple Vows, and afterwards went on to St. Mary's Priory, Bodmin for his novitiate, in the 1891 Population Census shows Hugh there with six other students, one of the six was a 17 year old called Phillip Corr, more of him later.

In October 1891 Abbot Felix Menchini (the Visitor), made a canonical visitation of St. Monica's Priory, and together with Augustine White, the Prior of Marnhull and Fr. John Higgins, gave out the "Tonsure & Minor Orders" to Rev. Francis Jeffrey, Rev. McGuiness, Rev. Brighton & Rev. Cotter, after which the Abbot went on to Bodmin to deal with the business of the house and to settle the differences which had arisen among the brethren there, they interviewed the eleven members in simple vows: these were in retreat to assess their situation and to decide whether or not they had a religious vocation. Four of the young men were dismissed as they were "lacking spirit and motive and so not called to religious life." One other (Hugh) just before he was about to make his solemn profession by taking his Solemn Vows at St. Monica's Priory, Spettisbury in Dorset, he was delayed for a year and was to told to remain in Bodmin, after which Hugh was dismissed by order of the Abbot General Felix Menchini, although I feel that Hugh had made up his mind to leave, Hugh left St Mary's Priory, in Bodmin in 1892. Abbot Felix Menchini remained in Bodmin until August the following year while the differences were sorted, Abbott Menchini suggested that Rev. John Cleary, Rev. Alipius Hughes, Rev. Maurice Suckling, and Rev. Edgar Sheldon should also leave the order.

During 1891 it seemed nobody was spared, Richard O'Regan, his simple vows were dispensed, on account of his ill health which rendered him unsuitable for religious life, William Carroll left Spettisbury when he received dispensation from his simple vows, also in 1891, John O'Connell and Stephen Lyons was banished home for several months for serious infringements of discipline, they later received dispensation from their simple vows and had gone by the end of 1891.

After only two years, Hugh had left the priesthood, the decision was possibly taken when Hugh was last at home in 1891, between himself and his future father-in-law, he followed John Ennis's advice, by joining the Allen Line the company he was Passenger Manager of,

Hugh had left the religious order on very good terms and kept in touch by letter and visits with the friends who had remained at St Mary's Priory in Bodmin. Philip John Henry Corr who was a 17 year old student and good friend of Hugh at St Mary's Priory, in Bodmin, was born about 1874 in Chardstock, Devon. He attended St. Joseph's Priory; Marnhull Juniorate (The first alumnate [or Juniorate] was established at Marnhull in Dorset in 1888) Philip took his Simple Vows before he left in 1890 for the Novitiate at St. Mary's Priory, Bodmin. In 1891 he went to St. Monica's Priory, Spettisbury where he made his solemn profession by taking his Solemn Vows in 1893. In September 1895 Bishop Graham came to St. Monica's Priory, for the ordinations of Rev. Holden, Rev. Donelan and Rev. Corr as sub-deacons. Later on the 29th September 1896, Bishop Graham came back to St. Monica's Priory, to celebrate an Ordination Mass, which, Rev. George McGregor and Rev. Wilfrid Regan were made sub-deacons and Gaudentius Holden and

Philip Corr, were made deacons. In 1902 Philip was transferred to Bodmin and in 1908 was sent to St Peter in Chains, Stroud Green in London, along with Edward Bovenizer.

Also in the 1891 Census, Hugh's sister, Charlotte, who was then 19 years of age, had taken a job, as a Governess, working for a General Practitioner William Orlagh and his wife, they had just moved from Manchester, to 48, Grange Wood Lodge, Ashby-de-la-Zouch, Bosworth near Leicester, to take up the position of GP in a larger practice that was well established, the surgery was next door at 49, Grange Wood Lodge.

Charlotte was to be Governess to their seven children (1 boy and 6 girls, their age ranging from 9 years to 12 months old), there was also four domestic servants, he had just taken up a new post as GP, after retiring from the Army Medical Corp as an Officer, Charlotte was given this position, because his wife Bertha was from Liverpool, and knew Charlotte's mother, Jessie, this was how positions where filled in those days, by arrangement.

In 1897, at the age of 20, Hugh's younger brother Richard on leaving his job in the Liverpool Dock Board (which is now part of the Mersey Docks and Harbour Board) attended St Francis College in Wimborne Minster, Dorsetshire, before entering the same order as Hugh, the Canons Regular and going onto St Mary's Priory, in Bodmin. In 1902 Richard was ordained as a priest at the age of 25.

When Richard was at Cotton Hall Preparatory School in 1885 he made a life time friend with another boarder who's name was Aloysuis (Alfred) Smith, neither knew at that time, that this friendship would last for the rest of their lives.

The Census Returns for Cotton College in 1881 shows:-

Aloysuis SMITH Boarder U Male 13 Birmingham, Warwick, England. Student

"Alfred" as Richard called him, because at the time he had a problem pronouncing his first name (because Richard spoke with a lisp), Aloysuis who was born in Weymouth, Dorset, as Walter James Smith, but spent his childhood in Birmingham, Warwickshire. He continued his education at the school of the Canons Regular in Rome and was ordained in 1897 after which he took his doctorate in theology.

Richard In 1898 he was a pupil at St. Joseph's Priory, Marnhull in Dorset and after his novitiate at St Mary's Priory, Bodmin in Cornwall in 1899, Richard then went onto St. Monica's Priory, Spettisbury where he made his solemn profession in 1904, both Richard and Aloysuis both renewed their friendship (from their early day's at Cotton College), it was Father Aloysuis Smith who travelled with Richard to Southampton on hearing of the disaster, because Father Aloysuis had a younger brother who was aboard R.M.S. Titanic, Reginald George Smith was a Saloon Steward.

When Father Aloysuis Smith arrived at St Mary's Bodmin in 1900, he held the position of "Prior", it was Reverend the Prior Aloysuis Smith CRL with the help from Richard who set up, with the help from the Sisters of Mercy, the first Catholic Convent at Bodmin in 1901, (It was the Sisters of Mercy who also ran St Joseph's Convent in Gosford Green, Coventry were Charlotte and Josephine attended for their convent education). Then in 1902 Richard and Aloysuis began a small catholic school, at Bodmin, but it was not until 1913 that Bodmin housed the Roman Catholic Orphanage and was the first of its kind to be set up in the West of England, the new Priory in Bodmin began in 1907, and in 1911 Father Richard McElroy would succeed Reverend the Prior Aloysuis Smith CRL as "Prior" of St Mary's RC Church in Bodmin, Cornwall, a post he held for many years. the reason for the succession of "Prior" was that Father Aloysuis Smith had been appointed as Visitor-General to the English Province and in 1914 he became a mitred abbot with the titular his roots, he was elected Abbot General, the first Englishman in the 500 year history of the order.

In 1952 he was enthroned as Abbot of Bodmin. He died on 20th Aug 1960 at Hayle and Abbot Aloysuis continued actively at Bodmin until a few years before his death, maintaining his interest in the work of the Order and particularly in the building of the abbey church at Bodmin which he saw sufficiently near to completion to look forward to pontificating at the first Mass, Father Aloysuis Smith died on Saturday 20th August 1960 in the hospital at Hayle, Cornwall, a large number of the Sisters of Mercy attended his funeral, he was buried in the same burial ground as Richard, at Bodmin.

In 1914 Hugh's brother Richard gave a lecture about the background to Bodmin Priory, his research dating back as far as 1193, the Priory had some distinguished sons, Robert Manning, the styled "Father of the English language", also two Archbishops of Canterbury were amongst it's cannons, but most of his lecture was taken up with "The foundation from Bodmin Priory and the Priory of Kells" (Kells in Kilkenny, Ireland). The lecture was about Bodmin Priory in the 12th century and how the cannons had worked in conjunction with the Knights, to secure a Priory in Kells. Richard, Earl of Strigul in 1193, founded the Priory of Kells, and the first cannons were from Bodmin Priory.

The big day in Hugh's life came when on Saturday 9th July 1910, at 3 o'clock, he married his long time sweetheart Miss Barbara Mary Ennis at St. Peters Church in Ballymitty, County Wexford in Ireland and the marriage was recorded at the Parish Church in Carrig-on-Bannow in 1910 (All the Parish marriages were registered there up to 1940), the marriage was witnessed by John Keogh, a Irishman that Hugh held in the highest esteem, it was also witnessed by Edith Ennis who was Barbara's younger sister, aged 31, from Hugh's family only his brother Richard attended the wedding, Hugh was then aged 35 and Barbara was aged 32, she was one of three children belonging to Mr. John J. Ennis J.P, formerly a Chief Purser and went on to be the Passenger Manager of the Allan Line. Hugh McElroy's brother, Reverend the Prior Richard McElroy RCL who had just recently been made Prior of St Mary's Priory in Bodmin, performed the marriage, Barbara's father presented St. Peters Church with a silver chalice to be used in the ceremony of Hugh and Barbara's marriage, the silver chalice remained in the church to this present day, and has been used in all their masses ever since, an item of great detail and beauty.

A sad day in 1942 Richard had been feeling very ill, he entered hospital for a slight operation but died 4 days later died and was buried at Bodmin. Abbot Aloysuis took the Mass, and a few years later, in 1960 Aloysuis passed away himself, now they would both be together again in the same burial ground in Bodmin, doing Gods work, the work they both loved.

Hugh had known Barbara when they were both growing up in Liverpool; and he often met Barbara at her father's office which was situated in Liverpool, Barbara's father had just moved to "Springwood" from 5, Derwent Road, West Derby in Liverpool, after his retirement, 5, Derwent Road is where incidentally Barbara, her sister Edith and brother John were born, their mother Elizabeth, was also born in Liverpool, she was 8 years younger than John Ennis her husband.

After their marriage, Hugh and Barbara lived with her father for a short while, because she wanted to spend as much time as she could with her farther, Mr. John J. Ennis, was a 75 year old widower, who shared the Family Estate and home with his younger brother Aidan Ennis (aged 70) who was a farmer, there was also sixteen other people who were accommodated in the house "Springwood", which was on the family estate, in Tullycanna, Ballymitty in Co. Wexford, which is situated about one mile along the Wexford Road from Ballymitty Church, John Ennis was by then a sick man and was cared for by a resident nurse, at his home (which would be considered a large house in those days) consisted of ten occupied rooms, also fifteen out offices (other buildings) and had nine windows at the front of the house, (the house is still the same today, nothing has changed, only the paint) it was run by domestic servants, the farming property also employed farmhands and a stableman, Hugh and Barbara stayed there just short of 12 months and then moved back to England, to the "Polygon" which is situated in, The Polygon, Southampton, at the time of the disaster they had been married for less than two years, (22 months to be exact) and there were no children to the marriage.

The Ennis Family no longer live in Springwood as there are now, no surviving members, Louise Ennis (who was Barbara's cousin) died in November 1987, aged 87, also Aidan Ennis, (son of Barbara's brother, John) who was a Jesuit priest, died in 2006 in Dublin, aged 93, a gentle and very caring man, who I had the privilege to meet in 2003, "Springwood" was sold soon after Louise died, to a John and Patience Nolan, who were from Rhodesia in Africa, John Nolan, would never allow "Springwood" to be photographed, for what ever his reasons were; I obtained six photos of "Springwood" for my research, that were approved by John Nolan.

I would at this point like to say a big thank you to Edna, for being a brilliant host when I stayed at "Springwood" in February 2007, (Edna was house-sitting for John & Patience Nolan who had just returned to Rhodesia for a holiday, while I was in Ballymitty), I was told, that it was strongly rumoured that some of the land at "Springwood" might be sold off for housing development and later "Springwood" may possibly go the same way.

Chapter 2

Seafaring Career

In 1892 Hugh McElroy commenced his seafaring career with the help of his future Father-in-Law, John Ellis, who before he fell ill, was the Passenger Manager of the Allan Line in Liverpool, where his family for two generations had been well known in shipping circles. Hugh went to sea for the first time in early 1893, as a Purser for the Allan Line on the R.M.S. Numidian, between Liverpool and Quebec, John Ellis must of thought highly of Hugh to put his Fleet's Chief Purser along with Hugh for his first voyage, to show him the rope's and pitfalls, but Hugh was said to of taken to it like a fish to water, he continued for the next 7 years, to serve the Allen Line in the same capacity in other vessels of their fleet, Hugh had reached his peak with the Allan Line, but wanted to make his own way to the top, after a long talk with John Ellis, his future Father-in-Law, Hugh's life from this point had been mapped out in front of him, following in John Ellis's footsteps, but not with the Allen Line, instead with White Star Line, because John Ellis knew and respected Bruce Ismay quite well, Hugh had been introduced to Bruce Ismay in 1898, by way of John Ellis, and in 1899 Hugh was offered the job of Purser with the White Star Line and was told to report to their Liverpool Office for induction into the company, his record of service with the Allen Line held him in good stead for those first few months.

Hugh's upbringing and education has taught him a very strict way of life, a new life has to be christened, in order to give it positive start in life, this brought Hugh into much conflict with the White Star Line, he was never given the reason why, their ships were never christened, when they were launched? Because the White Star Line were not in the business to discuss Thomas Ismay reasons for the aversion to the practice of christening his new ships, but the White Star fleet, from the original Oceanic through to the last ship built under White Star control, were never christened.

Thomas Henry Ismay personally made it crystal clear that no White Star ship would ever be christened, with Champaign or otherwise, because of the particular derivation of the ritual from ancient times. In fact, he never attended christenings of any ships, even of other lines, for that very same reason. He abhorred the practice. Bruce carried on his father's tradition of not christening White Star ships. Although both men were good Christians, as was Pirrie, Thomas Henry Ismay set the standard and it was simply followed. In fact, Thomas Henry Ismay politely and respectfully crossed swords with Queen Victoria over certain ships not being christened, especially the Teutonic which had been outfitted with guns in order to accommodate war efforts if ever drafted into service by the British Navy. Her upset was that a ship that might one day be requisitioned as a British Naval ship would not be properly christened. The Queen was one of the few people outside Thomas Henry Ismay's close circle who received the actual reason for his aversion, and as a result she acquiesced to his practice. "Them what runs the show, makes the rules".

Incidentally, it was rumoured that more than one White Star ship was unofficially christened by the men in the shipyards. Most of them were Irish, with some being Catholic and many being Protestant. Being Irish, they were often devout in their faith no matter how hot their tempers. Their beliefs were strong enough that they probably took it upon themselves to perform exofficio ceremonies on their own, albeit with cheap wine or beer and a group of at least partially inebriated workers. However, it was just as well that Thomas Henry Ismay did not find out about such goings on specifically because it could well have meant dismissal of the individuals involved, so strong was his aversion to the practice. Because of his respect and admiration for the workers, he probably tended to ignore rumours of this type and simply to be stern about not enjoining the practice officially.

Unlike his son, Thomas Henry Ismay felt rather close to the workers who would make his dreams come true. He had been raised on the docks and had a deep appreciation and love for the sea and the men who lived by her. He considered himself reasonably well-liked by employees of both White Star and Harland & Wolff, and he was probably correct in that assumption. His care for the men was expressed in a number of ways, not the least of which was for him to confer with division managers at the start of a yard tour and identify men with whom he could stop and chat and congratulate for their fine work. He had a knack for motivating people and the men seemed to appreciate it. However, after all was said and done he was still a member of the British upper class. Although he was known to share lunch at the yards with the workers, I do not believe any of them were ever invited to high tea at any of his homes. Had that ever become his practice, it is likely his wife Margaret would have laid down the law and put an end it in short order.

Hugh started his seafaring life with White Star on the R.M.S. Cymric and was quickly promoted to White Star liner S.S. Britannic one of the vessels, requisitioned into service by the British Government as a transport ship, transporting thousands of soldiers for the South African Boar War, troopship Britannic, during the Boer War, would carry some 37,000 troops to Africa, Hugh worked aboard S.S. Britannic with Captain Hayes who was then the commodore of the White Star Line, and later under the command of Captain E. J. Smith; who was decorated by King Edward VII with the Transport Medal for his position and service to the war effort, Hugh is mentioned in the "Boer War Transport Medal Roll" book, while serving aboard the S.S. Britannic, both Hugh and Captain E. J. Smith, were awarded the "Transport Medal" with the South Africa clasp, Hugh's medal was presented on 1st Dec 1903, by the Director of Transport, This medal was awarded to Pursers 'whose position and services specially deserved' on the reverse of the medal is the Latin inscription "OB PATRIAM MILITIBUS PER MARKE TRANSVECTI ADJUTUM" (For services rendered in transporting troops by sea).

It was after the Britannic became a military transport ship that McElroy ran across "Baden-Powell". The parrot arrived in Cape Town one day on a tramp steamer. McElroy was strolling along the docks having a rest from his military transport duties, when suddenly the air was rent with the cry, "Landlubber off the starboard" McElroy looked around and he caught the eye of the parrot, and then the feathered wonder piped, "He's rubbered."

Right then and there McElroy made up his mind to secure the bird and going on board the tramp steamer, he enquired for the owner. He was escorted to the cabin of one of the junior officers, who pleaded guilty to owning the bird. "I want him, and just simply have got to have him," was the way Britannics purser opened negotiations." Sorry but you can't have him," was the laconic refusal of the owner. Then McElroy worked on the officer's patriotism by telling him what a joy the bird would be to the thousands of soldiers who were destined to journey to and from England on the Britannic.

After some further negotiations the Officer gave in, "All right" he answered, "I will let you have him on one condition. His name now is Petroleum Pete, since Petroleum is what we carry principally, and I don't like that name, you must call him Baden-Powell," the bargain was concluded. Petroleum Pete was reregistered according to contract, and an hour later was safely caged away in McElroy's cabin aboard the Britannic, a few days later Hugh heard he was to be promoted Purser to the RMS Cedric, which would also be home for Baden-Powell, this was RMS Cedric's maiden voyage which was recorded by The New York Times, 21 February 1903.

LINER CEDRIC IN PORT

Largest Steamship Afloat Pronounced Steady as a Rock

Gales and High Seas Made No Impression on Her, and None of the Passengers Was Seasick

The largest steamship ever constructed slowly made her way, last evening between 6 and 8 o'clock, up New York Bay and the North River to the White Star piers at the foot of Bank Street. The huge vessel was the new transatlantic liner Cedric, a sister of the Celtic of the same fleet, but ninety-six tons larger.

The Cedric made a good voyage, according to officers and passengers, and each and every one of them pronounced her almost perfect as far as seaworthiness and easygoing in the roughest kind of weather are concerned. For instance, Sir Cavendish Boyle, the Governor of Newfoundland, who was among the passengers, said that she was as steady as a rock, and that although huge seas often hurled themselves against or over her sides, they had no effect on the monster, which went her way without even so much as a tremor. "The Cedric is a good example of the kind of ships the Morgan combine is turning out," added Sir Cavendish.

Another stanch supporter of the Cedric's qualities of resistance to big seas and high winds was Clegg, the White Star Line's veteran smoke-room steward, who has been in the employ of the line nearly a quarter of a century.

"When we left Queenstown," said Clegg, "I placed a small wine glass filled with champagne on the edge of a sideboard on the port side of the smoke room. I never touched that glass all the way across, and when we got to Sandy Hook to-day the glass had not moved half an inch and not a drop of wine had been spilled. Now, that proves that the Cedric is a wonder, doesn't it.

In appearance the Cedric is almost exactly like her sister ship the Celtic. What small differences in construction do exist, it would take an expert to find. She is 700 feet long, 75 feet wide, and has a depth of 49 1-3 feet. Her gross tonnage is 21,000 tons, while her displacement is 38,000 tons. Like the Celtic, she has four masts and two funnels, and is designed to cross the Atlantic at an average speed of about 17 knots. Her interior fittings, while not at all gorgeous, are yet elegant in appearance.

The Cedric brought 742 passengers, 312 of whom were in the first and second cabin. According to Dr. R. D. Doble, formerly of the Teutonic, the ship's surgeon, not a passenger was seasick during the voyage, so easily did the big ship plough her way through the mountainous seas on the way over. The log of the liner show's that she encountered all kinds of gales, especially during the last four days, when she ran into a succession of heavy northwesters.

"They did not bother us any, though," said Capt. Haddock, "for on this ship you would hardly know you were at sea unless you happened to take a walk on deck or looked out of your stateroom window."

The Cedric crossed the ocean in 8 days, 8 hours, and 16 minutes. She came over the long course of 2,889 miles from Daunt's Rock to New York, and her log shows that her day's runs were 365, 390, 383, 333, 351, 331, 303, 358, and 75 to Sandy Hook. Her average speed was 14 1/2 knots.

Her commander is Capt. H. J. Haddock, C. B; R. N. R., formerly of the Britannic, Germanic and Celtic. The chief officer is Lieut. Alexander Hambleton, R. N. R., and the chief engineer J. W. Alexander, who for the last two years had been chief engineer on the Britannic, which has been doing service as a Government transport. The purser is H. McElroy.

Sir Cavendish Boyle said he would go to Montreal to-day, where he would try and open communication with his Government. He feared, he said, that it would be hard to do so, owing to the damage to telegraph wires and navigation by storms and ice, and added that he might be compelled to go to Halifax to catch a boat to take him to St. John's. Others on board were H. Montague Allen, Sir Randolph Baker, T. P. Burnham, Capt. James Cole, R. N.; G. L. Davidson, Erastus S. Day, United States Consul at Bradford; Capt. C. D. Falbes, Richard McCreery, and J. Robertson.

Funston" the famous Mexican parrot of Castle William on Governors Island, has there been seen in these parts a bird so wonderfully intelligent as is Baden-Powell, the big white Australian parrot whose home is on the White Star liner SS Cedric. The other day when the SS Cedric sailed out of New York bound for Liverpool on her return maiden voyage, there stood at the rail waving farewell to friends ashore a big well-built man named McElroy and on his shoulder there perched a great white parrot, McElroy is SS Cedric's purser and Baden-Powell is his ward.

When the SS Cedric arrived in New York on her last trip Baden-Powell was not on deck when the big liner was berthed neither was his guardian. When found he was perched on McElroy's shoulder, the officer being busy in his office getting his papers ready to be turned over to the proper officials. An acquaintance of McElroy knocked at the door." Keep out. No lobsters wanted", is what the knocker on the outside heard from within, "Shut up, Baden, Come in it's alright" answered McElroy, and the friend opened the door. McElroy greeted his friend warmly while Baden-Powell with a look of disdain on his pealed countenance eyed him critically.

"Bum-looker, don't eat much ice," piped the parrot. McElroy told the bird to shut up and where upon Baden-Powell gave a loud "All right, all right" and leaving his place on McElroy shoulder, took up his position on the windowsill overlooking the grand stairway. "Look out Mac; the old man's coming!" said Baden-Powell", I told you to shut up retorted the purser; "All right answered Baden-Powell and obeyed orders.

Hugh's record of service with the White Star Line is unique; he served them for some thirteen years, and had served first on board the R.M.S. Cymric and then the troopship S.S. Britannic, during the Boer War, Hugh worked aboard HMT.S. Britannic with Captain Hayes who was then the commodore of the White Star Line, and later served under Captain E. J. Smith; and then he was promoted Purser to the R.M.S. Cedric, then R.M.S. Baltic and then Hugh was to be promoted Purser to the R.M.S. Majestic.

While Hugh was later serving on the R.M.S. Cedric in August 1904, as the Purser, on the New York to Liverpool route, James Kearney who worked as (Mate) Deck Officer, when she arrived in Southampton, James had invited Lucinda his wife and Mary her sister to visit his ship, James introduced them to the Purser who was a friend of his, Purser McElroy on learning that Mary was from Liverpool and also a music teacher, asked her what she would like the orchestra to play and she chose The Merry Widows waltz which he then asked the orchestra to play. (Una, Mary's daughter remembers that when she was a child, whenever that piece of music would come on the radio her mother could not listen to it and would leave the room in tears). James and Hugh first met in the White Star Lines offices in Liverpool when Hugh was having his induction into the company and also aboard the R.M.S. Cedric.

It was reported in The Washington Post, Friday February 16th 1906, that Cuba are to present a wedding present to Miss Alice Roosevelt the President of America's daughter, who is to marry Mr Nicholas Longworth. The wedding present is a splendid pearl necklace costing about $25,000 and manufactured by a firm of Parisian jewellers, in France. They should arrived today aboard the White Star liner R.M.S. Majestic, in charge of the wedding present is purser McElroy, who had received it from a representative of the American Express Company at Liverpool for transportation to Washington D.C.

The package containing the necklace was bound with cord and sealed with six wax seals. A seal on one corner was slightly cracked, and the cord was a bit loose when the package was handed over to Customs Inspector Moore, in New York, just after the liner docked, He viewed it with unusual circumspection, and discovering the slight crack was naturally anxious to have so precious a thing as a package containing a gift to the daughter of the President in proper shape when it left his hands, and insisted that it should be weighed.

According to the bill of lading the weight of the package when it was shipped was six pounds one and one-half ounces. It was put on a pair of scales on the pier for weighing bulky material, and apparently was one and a half pounds less than the bill of lading called for; Moore believed that the package had been tampered with. (The man was obviously scared), so the Customs Dept then had the package weighed at the office of the express company and showed not a variation of a fraction of an ounce from the weight named on the bill of lading.

The package was dispatched to Washington D.C. in the care of a special messenger who will turn it over to the Cuban Minister. The Foreign Manager, Mr Berry, of the express company, said there was no doubt that the necklace was all right, and that there been no attempt to tamper with the package. The bill of lading read: "To His Excellency the Minister of Cuba, No. 1000, Sixteen Street, Washington, D.C. "One case containing a box with six red pearls of the Cuban consul in Paris: one pearl necklace, value, 128,175 francs, no duty being imposed, Received from the Minister of Cuba in Paris, bound to Georgetown D.C; insurance, $81.96; weighing six pounds one and one-half ounces."

Another incident happened in mid-Atlantic on the R.M.S. Majestic, Monday, 22nd October 1906, while Hugh was serving as Purser, again under command of Captain Hayes, which was reported in the New York Times on the 25th October 1906.

RUNAWAYS WED IN MID OCEAN

A Romantic Marriage of Swedish Immigrants on the Majestic

"Passengers on the White Star Liner 'Majestic' which arrived yesterday afternoon witnessed in mid-Atlantic the wedding of two Swedish immigrants. The happy couple were Wilfred Larsen and Elizabeth Wickstrand both natives of Bronten, Sweden, the Rev. Robert C. Williams performed the ceremony last Monday morning in Purser McElroy's Office. The entry in the official log book was signed, as witnessed by Senator W. A. Clark of Montana, USA and Mr J. E. Hargreaves, Justice of the Peace of Westmoreland, England, who were both to witnesses the marriage also Captain Hayes of the 'Majestic'. After the Wedding the newly wedded pair had a reception in the saloon, a toast to their health and future prosperity was proposed by Senator Clark and drunk by the passengers. A wedding cake had been prepared for the occasion by the ship's chief baker C. Russell and a purse was subscribed by the salon passengers and given to the bridegroom. The compatriots of the couple in the steerage kept the fun up till the early hours on Tuesday morning".

What interested everybody aboard was the romance of the match. Both Larsen and Wickstrand were sweethearts from childhood in Bronten, Sweden. Their parents opposed the match, so they made up their minds to run away to America and get married. Some of their friends on board the R.M.S. Majestic suggested that there might be an order to stop them on arrival at Ellis Island, so they decided to be married at sea and land in America as man and wife. Captain Hayes who had twenty four years experience in the White Star service said this was the first time he had witnessed a marriage on the Atlantic, on a short trip from Liverpool to New York.

"On arrival in New York the happy pair was accepted by the immigration authorities on our explaining what had happened and being shown the official entry in the Majestic's Official Log concerning the matter. They were told to call at the British Consulate for their marriage certificate after they had been passed through Ellis Island".

Captain Hayes stated "A photograph was taken afterwards on the saloon deck by Dr Francis the doctor of the R.M.S. Majestic, with my camera and when I later looked for the film, I found it had been taken from the camera by the doctor and sold to a New York newspaper, the photograph appeared in the press the next morning 25th October 1906, after we arrived".

It is this newspaper account of the ceremony and more so the photograph, that I have been searching for, it has become the missing link, so to speak, along with the help of Newspaper Heritage Microfilm and Newspaper Archive of America, and have to-date only found one account, in the New York Times, (with no photograph) my research will continue until we discover that missing photograph hopefully of Hugh on the saloon deck of the R.M.S.. Majestic, (over twelve months later, the photograph was located on 4th April 2009 in The Anaconda Standard from Montana, USA. 9th November 1906 – Friday Morning edition, Hugh was not part of the photo, because he had taken it).

It was reported in The New York Times on Friday December 21st 1906, that the White Star liner R.M.S. Majestic which arrived in New York on Thursday 20th December 1906 from England,

and had brought 4,570 sacks of mail and 85 bags of parcel post, this according to Purser McElroy, is the record for mail carried on a single vessel, the R.M.S. Majestic also brought $200,000 in specie.

With regards to getting married aboard the "R.M.S. Majestic", seems to of started something amongst the young immigrants, before being passed through Ellis Island, because two years later, an article appeared again with regards to getting married onboard liners, in the New York Times on the 9th October 1908.

The club that the three couples formed the "Majestic club" only held one reunion meeting, and then it seemed to of fizzled-out.

THREE COUPLES WED ON THE MAJESTIC

Immigration Law Unearths a Series of Romances When the Liner Arrives

GIRLS CAME HERE TO MARRY

Not Allowed to Land, So a Parson Tied the Knot on the Ship and the Officers Gave Them a Breakfast.

The White Star liner Majestic, which arrived from Southampton, late Wednesday, was the scene of a triple wedding yesterday. A curious feature of the ceremony was that the three brides never met until they boarded the Majestic and the three bridegrooms had never heard of each until they met in the saloon of the liner on Wednesday.

Among the second class passengers were three young English girls, each of whom told the immigration officials that they had come here to marry. They were Miss Alice L. Osborne of Norwich, who was betrothed to Walter R. Smith, formerly of London, but now the New York representative of an English machinery firm; Miss Mildred Hand of Bournemouth, England, who was to wed Ernest Dower, who used to live in Fordham Bridge, England, but is now a clerk for the Interborough Railroad, and Miss Rose Jane Webb of Portsmouth, England, who as the wife of Eno Deason will live in Cleveland, Ohio.

It had been the intention of Mr. Smith and Miss Osborne to marry at the home the former has established at 502 West 172nd Street, but when he learned that the Government exercised a care over young women landing here he consented to be married in the saloon of the Majestic. The situation was explained to the other two men and they agreed to be married on board. So the ship's officers and the stewards, being interested in the triple event, set out to prepare a celebration.

It was necessary before the ceremony to make a trip to the License Bureau at the City Hall, and so the happy couples were taken there under the chaperonage of Mrs. Walters, the Ellis Island matron.

The three were married by the Rev. Jacob Price of the Washington Heights Methodist Episcopal Church.

Purser Edwards gave the brides in marriage, and after the ceremony the party sat down to a wedding breakfast which had been spread in the saloon. After it was over the three couples made a tour of the city in a sight-seeing automobile. They also agreed that they would form themselves into a Majestic club with the object of holding a reunion once a year.

To an inquirer who sought their stories Miss Osborne said that she first met Mr. Smith in Yarmouth, England, and fell in love with him because of his rowing. Miss Webb said that she met Mr. Deason while visiting her sister and Miss Hand said that she met Mr. Dower so long ago that really she had forgotten [sic] just how it all happened.

Hugh was rapidly promoted as new and larger liners were added to the fleet (the introduction of Hugh to Bruce Ismay by way of John Ennis and in the proving himself to be a good Purser had helped him immensely and Bruce Ismay was not a man to throw a good hand of poker away, as it was mentioned in the evidence of trust and confidence reposed in him, that he took the maiden voyages successively in the R.M.S.. Cedric and the R.M.S. Republic which opened the Boston/Mediterranean service, the vessel which, it may be remembered, later she foundered in Mid-Atlantic, though all hands were happily saved though the instrumentality of wireless telegraphy, also the R.M.S. Baltic who sailed from Liverpool on 29th June 1904, stopping the next day at Queenstown to pick up mails and passengers. She is in the command of Lieut. E. J. Smith, R.N.R; The R.M.S. Baltic is the tenth command which Lieut. Smith has held in the service of the White Star Line.

The Officers of the R.M.S. Baltic were Thomas Kidwell, formerly the chief officer of the Celtic; W. E. Graham surgeon; H. McElroy purser, and H. Wovenden chief steward. And to commemorate her maiden voyage the ship will be open for public inspection in New York on Monday 11th July 1904 and an admission fee of 25 cents will be asked from each visitor, the proceeds to go to the seamen's charities.

Hugh also later served on the R.M.S. Adriatic, he was so popular with the passengers is amply borne out by extracts from periodicals published. The writer of the "Motley Notes" in the "Daily Sketch" of 24th April 1911 makes the following reference. "When I crossed from New York to Plymouth on the R.M.S. Adriatic just before Christmas, 1910, McElroy was the Chief Purser of that vessel, I described McElroy very briefly in these notes; here is the description: "Seven of us" I wrote, "sit together at meals, and I fancy we are the merriest table in the salon. At the head sits one of the chief officers. He is so modest a fellow that I will forbear to name him; but let me hint that he is famous among all those who go down to the sea in ships as a first class raconteur' . . . . Big, jolly, courteous, human to the last inch", McElroy was the ideal man for the position he held".

It was reported in the Fort Wayne Sentinel, USA on the July 1910 that Purser Hugh McElroy of the R.M.S. Adriatic had once again taken to Parrot Minding, the following article along with a picture of Hugh holding the parrot. Appeared in the New York Times on the 28th July 1910.

FEATHERED "JACK BINNS" SENDS WIRELESS MESSAGE

Mr Joseph Finley tells of wonderful parrot he found in Hartz Mountains—Began by imitating finger taps on table—Then learns to tap the operator's key and send messages out from the SS. Adriatic

"Mr Joseph Finley, at his home in 494, Hulsey Street, Brooklyn, today told the story of his capture of the wonderful parrot that will arrive here sometime this week and which is now sending wireless messages with unerring aim all over the Atlantic. Mr Finley arrived on the White Star line steamship "Cedric" with two friends.

"I caught my parrot in the Hartz mountains." said Mr Finley. "He had escaped from some zoological garden in Germany. Undoubtedly, but as I could not discover the owner I kept the bird and found, after a few days, that he would imitate the taps I made on the table with my fingers, a habit I have. Later, in London, I met Mr McElroy, who is the Purser of the "Adriatic" I gave him the parrot and telling him the trick of the parrot of imitating the tapping of my fingers, it was found that he would tap the wireless key on the Adriatic just as regularly and precisely as he did the table tap".

"As a result of some experiments, the parrot was found quite competent to send wireless messages without the regular operator touching the key, the bird simply following each tap of the operator's finger on the table with a tap on the key. He was quite precise in his imitation of the dots and dashes, and I was highly gratified in getting a wireless message on the "Cedric" which was sent "via McElroy's parrot, as the message stated."

According to Mr Finley the parrot he caught will become a second "Jack Binns" if he keeps on at the rate that he is now going. The taps on the table of the Adriatic's wireless operator's finger were instantly copied by the "wireless parrot" and repeated on the key controlling the sending of the wireless dispatches by the bird striking the key with its foot.

Advance news of the "Adriatic" may be expected today or tomorrow, providing, of course, that Purser McElroy's parrot is in his usual good form.

"Jack Binns" was the Marconi wireless operator onboard The R.M.S.. Republic, at the time of her sinking 23rd January 1909, during the collision of the Florida with the Republic. Binns was hailed a hero in sending CDQ and saving everyone onboard, and in 1910 was assigned to R.M.S. Adriatic, where his captain is E.J. Smith, and in 1911 he should have been assigned to the Olympic and then the Titanic with E.J. Smith (as part of the team), but J. Bruce Ismay, head of the White Star Line, is worried that he might bring bad luck and bad publicity to these new ships. Therefore Jack Binns was assigned first to the S.S. Caronia and then to the S.S. Minnewaska, and also receives the post of traveling inspector, created for him by the White Star Line. In 1912 he resigns from the Marconi company to work for William Randolph Hearst at the New York American. Two days after he begins his new career, the Titanic strikes an iceberg and sinks. He reports extensively on the disaster for the New York American. He also testifies at the Titanic inquiry himself.

Hugh was transferred from the "R.M.S. Adriatic" along with Chief Steward Latimer and Dr O'loughlin to serve aboard R.M.S. Olympics for her maiden voyage, Hugh was to be part of a team and work alongside Purser Claude Lancaster for her maiden voyage. Lancaster had sailed with Captain Haddock for a very long time, got along with him quite well and was more or less his purser. So Lancaster was preparing himself with training on the job aboard the R.M.S.

Olympic for the time when he would rejoin Captain Haddock who was hopefully to take over the R.M.S. Titanic.

Hugh McElroy's choice as R.M.S. Olympics other purser is also very telling, because the purser is the most senior non-executive officer. He is, or should be, the master's confidante in all shipboard, social and political matters; the passengers use to ask the pursers for advice and expected that the pursers were familiar with the vessel. A ship on her first voyage was consistently a nightmare to pursers as they did not know the ship very well themselves. In the case of the R.M.S. Olympic, nothing could be done about it, but in the case of the R.M.S. Titanic, it certainly would have been remedied.

Captain Smith was expected to retire before R.M.S. Titanic was put into service, considering that it had taken seven months from launch to completion of the R.M.S. Olympic, a completion of the R.M.S. Titanic within seven months of her launch should be regarded as possible. Launching day was 31st May 1911, seven months from then on would make 31st December 1911. Smith's birthday was in January and he would then be aged 62 in 1912, taking the R.M.S. Olympic on her maiden voyage and commanding her until retiring in either December 1911 or even January 1912 sounds quite consistent, but with Smith retiring, even Captain Haddock would get the chance to command the R.M.S. Olympic before eventually taking over R.M.S. Titanic and then Bertram Hayes was to be put in charge of the R.M.S. Olympic.

The advantage of this situation would have been the following: R.M.S. Titanic would have a master who had already commanded the R.M.S. Olympic and some of her crew would also have served aboard the sister ship before thus gaining experience with this class of vessels. And Bertram Hayes being inexperienced with the size of these liners would get aboard a vessel with a large part of the crew already accustomed to the ship and their duties, Wilde and Murdoch were to work together and managed to do so. In fact, the crew referred to Murdoch as the "Junior Chief" which indicates that he, although being 1st officer according to the crew agreement, was further adapting to the duties of a Chief Officer. It had been said that Wilde and Murdoch had something in common: Both of them knew that their present master, Captain Edward John Smith, was blocking their respective promotion as long as he did not retire.

Captain E. J. Smith's replacement purser aboard "R.M.S. Adriatic" was A. B. Appleyard, who was about Hugh McElroy's age, while Hugh had chiefly been with Captain Bertram Fox Hayes, (a favourite Captain of Captain Hewitt, and the White Star Head Marine superintendent). This being so, there is one obvious reason for this decision: Bertram Fox Hayes should take over the R.M.S. Olympic when Smith eventually retired. The latter's retirement would also make Captain Herbert J. Haddock to the most senior White Star captain, hence he would then become R.M.S. Titanic's master.

On the return maiden voyage of the R.M.S. Olympic, there was something not quite straight forward, Hugh never gave out details to anyone, of any important passengers that had booked passage, even if they were travelling incognito, Mrs. William K. Vanderbilt, Jr; and her three children were among the passengers. She was booked as "Mrs. Vincent", (Mrs Anne Vanderbilt), who made her way to her stateroom at the last minute, and appeared to be surprised that her presence aboard was known. She would say nothing regarding her plan's, she was asked why she had booked passage as "Mrs. Vincent." She smiled and said, "I never submit to an interview." The children occupied the imperial suite and Mrs. Vanderbilt the suite next adjoining.

After the R.M.S. Olympic, Hugh was transferred to the R.M.S. Titanic. He signed on the R.M.S. Titanic on the evening of Tuesday 9th April 1912 as Chief Purser on a salary of £20 per month, it was said that Purser McElroy, Chief Steward Latimer and Dr O'loughlin were all part of the Smith "crowd". they were all crew members that Captain Smith certainly wanted to have, serving with him, both as subordinates and as friends, Captain E.J. Smith had enough pull with White Star to effect keeping them with him on board the R.M.S. Olympic and R.M.S. Titanic the only other persons with a greater salary were Chief Officer Henry Wilde who's earnings was £25 per month and Captain Smith who's estimated salary was £105 per month, Chief Officer Henry Wilde was also to be became a member of the Smith "crowd", although his transfer to R.M.S. Titanic was never fully explained.

White Star Line

Special Meeting April 10th 1912
Minute No. 8424

"Having fitted out this magnificent vessel, the R.M.S. Titanic, we proceeded to man her with all that was best in the White Star organization, and that, I believe, without boasting, means everything in the way of skill, manhood and esprit de corps. Whenever a man had distinguished himself in the service by means of ability and devotion to duty, he was earmarked at once to go to the R.M.S. Olympic or R.M.S. Titanic, if it were possible to spare him from his existing position, with the result that, from Captain Smith, Chief Engineer Bell, Dr. O'Loughlin, Chief Purser McElroy, Chief Steward Latimer, downwards, I can say without fear of contradiction, that finer set of men never manned a ship, nor could be found in the whole of the Mercantile Marine of the country and no higher testimony than this can be paid to the worth of any crew".

Joseph Bruce Ismay

Chapter 3

The Expectations of Titanic

Hugh had sent two postcards from the Royal Southampton Yacht Club, both were to his priest friends one to Phillip Corr dated 6th April 1912 it read as follows: "Many thanks for your letter and good wishes which I reciprocate, the R.M.S. Titanic is in many ways an improved R.M.S. Olympic and will I trust be a success, I am sorry I could not get down to Swanage this time but I was tied to Southampton and the train service too erratic to take chances, all kind of messages to you both". On the card which still exists, in a different hand had noted "coal strike time" against the reference to the train service and so the R.M.S. Titanic sailed. The other card was to his close friend Cuthbert McAdam still in Bodmin Priory; this was also dated 6th April 1912 with a message in a similar vein.

By a strange coincidence, Hugh had made the acquaintance of a Mr Octavio Biet whom Hugh found to be very trustworthy, he was a business man from Valletta in Malta, while they were both staying at the "Polygon" in Southampton, Hugh and Barbara along with Mr Octavio Biet had received Holy Communion on the Sunday 7th April before Titanic's maiden voyage, coincidently neither Hugh nor Mr Octavio Biet, knew that they both had attended the same school, "Cotton Hall Ecclesiastical College",(because Mr Octavio Biet left Cotton Hall College in 1903)

Hugh had arranged to sent a bouquet of flowers, (which were red and white, the Danish national colours) to the world famous Danish dancer "Mdlle Adeline Genee", to be delivered backstage, prior to her special "Flying Matinee" performance at the Hippodrome Theatre in Southampton on the Thursday 11th April 1912 at 2.30 p.m; she was a friend of both Hugh and Barbara, the friendship first began when Hugh made her acquaintance aboard the R.M.S. Majestic on route to America, Barbara did go and see Mdlle Adeline Genee in her special performance, Hugh had suggested to Mr Octavio Biet, if he would possibly escort Barbara to attend the special performance at the Hippodrome Theatre, in Southampton as Mdlle Adeline Genee had sent Hugh two complimentary tickets. Mr Octavio Biet asked Barbara if that would be in order, and she accepted his invitation, with Hugh's blessing, Hugh left the "Polygon" on Tuesday evening, to go and stay aboard R.M.S. Titanic, as he had a mountain of business to attend, and arrange, before R.M.S. Titanic maiden voyage at mid-day the next day Wednesday 10th April 1912.

Hugh staying aboard R.M.S. Titanic the night before her maiden voyage, would mean he had the chance to meet an old friend, the purser from the SS Lanrentic, Geoffrey P. Rogers, who was to be his assistant purser, this was arranged by White Star, but at the last moment this was cancelled and another old friend, Reg Baker; late of the R.M.S. Majestic, was ordered to the R.M.S. Titanic, Hugh would also meet with all the Purser's assistants, Ernest King, Reg Rice, Ashcroft and Donald Campbell, to get things sorted before any crew or passengers boarded the R.M.S. Titanic the next day, it was a coincidence that Baker relieved Rogers, when the latter left the Republic, Baker's life was spared when the disaster overcame the Republic, but only to lose it while employed on the R.M.S. Titanic.

Marcoigrams signal was sent to the Canadian Pacific liner "Empress of Britain", 12th April 1912 which was eastbound from Halifax to Liverpool and reads "Fishwick, Purser, Empress of Britain, Thanks, kindest regards, all going well, McElroy" the reply was a Marconigram received by R.M.S. Titanic on the 12th April 1912 at 1.43 p.m. from "Empress of Britain" reads "Purser McElroy, R.M.S. Titanic, Congratulations and good luck, Fishwick". Hugh's friendship with Purser Fishwick goes back to his early childhood days in Liverpool.

Stewards were given their printed list of names, 1st Class Steward, William Faulkner read the words "First Class Passenger List, per Royal and US Mail". The Staterooms of those of whom he had responsibility had been ticked with a pencil mark by Chief Purser Hugh McElroy.

Purser Hugh McElroy suddenly appeared at Faulkner's side. He was accompanied by a passenger who wanted a cabin other than that allocated. Mr Howard B. Case, an oil magnate with interest on both sides of the Atlantic, had been given accommodation down on E deck (E66), he was none too pleased. He had specifically asked for C deck (C11) and wanted to switch cabins, even if it meant sacrificing space, the Purser had found one more cabin which might conform to Mr Cases liking, Hugh handed the Steward his note of authorization for the changeover and asked him to attend to the matter personally, Faulkner read the note, pocketed it and carried out the instruction, which lead to another happy passenger.

Purser McElroy checked the day's receipt from the bars and the Marconi room before placing them in his safe. He noted the special packages in the vault, given into his personal keeping, instead of being consigned to the cargo holds. "Nothing special he mused, he leafed through his own copy of the cargo manifest . . . . Nor here . . . Just routine express cargo . . . certainly nothing that is heavily insured, no instructions for special handling, either, well one good thing it will not take long to unload" he folded the manifest and placed it back into the safe with the package list. He closed and locked the safe door, after minding a Mr Finley's parrot ("Jack Binns") aboard the R.M.S. Adriatic's, Hugh had now taken to canary minding, the canary sailed on the R.M.S. Titanic and survived, it was owned by a Mr. Meanwell who lived in Carentan, France and wanted to get his prize winning precious canary to Cherbourg from England. He asked the Chief Purser to carry it on R.M.S. Titanic, and to have the bird in his office, the canary disembarked when the R.M.S. Titanic arrived in Cherbourg, after securing his Office; he crossed the first class forward entrance and went towards his own unmarked cabin next door to C53.

R.M.S. Titanic arrives at Cherbourg, France, at 6.30 p.m. R.M.S. Titanic drops anchor and the Two White Star tenders, "S.S. Traffic" carrying third class passengers plus all the mail, was the first to come alongside, carrying 102 third class passengers, next to come alongside was "S.S. Normadic", she was carrying 144 first class passengers and 26 Second Class, which included among it's passengers, the Astor's, Widener's, Spedden's and Thayer also Molly Brown and Mrs Geneviève Cassebeer, to name just a few, also aboard S.S. Normadic were 26 second class passengers, making a total of 272 passengers to come aboard,. R.M.S. Titanic didn't remain in Cherbourg any longer than was needed to drop off and pick up some passengers; dinner aboard R.M.S. Titanic was delayed and would be served after the ship left the port of Cherbourg at 9.00pm sailing down the English Channel heading towards the Southern coast of Ireland.

Purser McElroy averred on the R.M.S. Titanic as he did aboard the R.M.S. Olympic, that the daily tour of inspection, which he made at 10:30 a.m. with Captain Smith, Dr. O'Loughlin, and Chief Steward Latimer, was beginning to tell on him. The Captain would computed the distance, while the surgeon insisted that it seemed more like nine miles, Captain Smith would say "come on boys, stride to it".

Father Browne visited the Pursers Office to see the Chief Purser McElroy and to give him a letter of introduction, this served as a passport to Father Browne, which made way to the genial friendship between Purser McElroy and Father Browne, the author of this letter was a old friend of the Chief Purser, The Most Rev Dr Robert Browne, Bishop of Cloyne, Queenstown (Cobh). Bishop Browne who was Father Francis Browne's uncle and had just won a libel case against the Dundee Courier for £200.

The Bishop did not need the money, so he paid for the two day passage on the R.M.S. Titanic and also for a brand new camera for his nephew, Father Browne certainly was in debt to R.M.S. Titanic's Purser, Hugh McElroy, because as purser he had given Father Browne the run of the ship, purser's are responsible for all accommodations on shipboard, and Hugh could have thrown open any room he wished, within reason, we know that Father Browne travelled throughout the ship, and not just in first class. We now know he paid extensive visits to second class and steerage accommodation, also to the Transatlantic Post Office, also the Marconi Room and the Purser's Office and many other places. If the priesthood had not relinquished its claim on Hugh McElroy, he would not have known Bishop Browne, and if it was not for Father Browne's letter of introduction, the world of R.M.S. Titanic would be very much the poorer.

The R.M.S. Titanic's Pursers Office was arranged on two decks, "C" deck would consist of the Chief Purser's own office and a large enquiry office, and also Hugh had his own cabin which was next to C53, on "C" Deck starboard of the first class forward entrance.

On E" Deck it would include the Second Class or Assistant Purser's Office, which was located on "E" deck opposite the Aft Staircase, which was organized by the 40 year old Assistant Purser Reginald L. Baker, this was next to his own cabin, and the Purser's clerks office which was about 20 feet to the starboard side of the Aft Staircase, this office was run by the 28 year old Pursers Clerk Ernest W. King, along with 28 year old Mr John Reginald Rice, 26 year old Mr A. Ashcroft and 28 year old Mr Donald S. Campbell.

At 11.30 a.m. on Thursday 11th April, the liner drops anchor off Queenstown harbour, about two miles from the coastline, she is flanked by the tenders "S.S. America" and "S.S. Ireland", which also belong to the White Star Line. 113 emigrants travelling steerage plus 1,385 sacks of mail [according to the ships passenger list and manifest] came aboard that day, along with local reporters who were invited to come aboard and look round the great liner, as their French and English counterparts have already done. In those days, newspapers fulfilled the same function that the radio and television does today. Consequently, they were an extremely powerful means of communication and advertising. To avoid conflicting stories, the White Star Line had taken great care to maintain excellent relationships with reporters in different countries. The reporter's descriptions of the R.M.S. Titanic and the R.M.S. Olympic could guarantee the success of the two vessels. To add to the activity, without warning, several small boats loaded with Irish lace and fabric drew alongside the embarkation gangways. After seeking permission, the owners are allowed on board as an exceptional matter, and for a short while the decks of the R.M.S. Titanic were transformed into a luxuriously coloured market.

The Chief Executive of the White Star Line, Mr Joseph Bruce Ismay knew the importance and the power of the media, whilst the reporters were aboard reporting on the "R.M.S. Titanic". Captain E. J. Smith along with Chief Purser Hugh McElroy, were assisting one reporter Mr Thomas Baker a reporter/photographer from the Cork Examiner on the Officers Promenade deck after he had made his notes he asked if he could take a photo, and had them both pose outside Captain Smith's Quarters on the Officers Promenade, on the starboard side, Hugh had some reservations about having his photo taken aboard the R.M.S. Titanic he thought it had sinister connotations, after Thomas Baker had finished taking his photo, Father Browne asked if possible, could he take a similar photo of Hugh and Captain Smith, at this point Hugh was more relaxed and it is borne in the photo Father Brown took, which is now possibly more famous than the photo taken by Mr Thomas Baker, although all the photo's taken by Father Francis Browne (who later became a Jesuit priest) where destined to become famous throughout the world, as they were the last images to be recorded aboard the R.M.S. Titanic, it seems strange that only Father Browne had a camera aboard R.M.S. Titanic, especially for her maiden voyage.

Now, with Queenstown and the Irish coast rapidly fading on the horizon, R.M.S. Titanic moved out into the open waters of the Atlantic Ocean. The crew and officers could now begin to get into their routines and watches, and the passengers now had time to explore the great liner, meet old cruising friends, or organise parties for the rich and the famous.

Mrs. Imanita Shelley and her mother, Mrs. Lutie Davis Parrish, of Woodford County, Kentucky., embarked on the R.M.S. Titanic at Southampton, England on the 10th April, 1912, having purchased second-class accommodation aboard the R.M.S. Titanic, as soon as they were accommodated, Mrs. Lutie Davis Parrish sent the stewardess to the Chief Purser, demanding transfer to the accommodation she had purchased. Purser McElroy replied he could do nothing until R.M.S. Titanic had left Queenstown, Ireland, when he would check up all tickets and find out if there was any mistake.

After R.M.S. Titanic had left Queenstown, Mrs. L. D. Parrish made 11 trips herself to the Chief Pursers Office asking him for a transfer, only to be put off with promises, and at 9 p.m; no one having come to take them to their requested accommodation, Mrs. Shelley wrote a note to the purser to the effect that she had paid for the best second-class accommodation on the ship and had the receipts to prove it, she was also very ill and, owing to the freezing cold of the cabin, was in great danger; that if he, the purser, refused to act, she, Mrs. Shelley, would appeal to the captain, and if neither would act she realized she would have to wait until reaching America for redress, but most assuredly would claim damages, if she should ever reach her native land. The result of this letter was the arrival of four stewards to carry both her and her mother's luggage to the room paid for (second-class), and the stewards offered apology after apology.

The purser first asked the stewardess on reading the note, "If they were really so very sick", to which she answered "there was no doubt about that". Then the purser asked her "if there was such a cabin on board the R.M.S. Titanic, where a cabin trunk could not be opened", which she replied that she did not think so. One of the stewards, also told him that "the cabin was entirely too small for two women, and that it was too small for two men, it was impossible for himself or anyone else to enter the cabin and to wait upon the occupants unless both of them first climbed into their berths". The purser then told the steward that he "would have to act at once, or the company would get into trouble".

29

The weather on the morning of Friday April 12th 1912 was fine, but yet chilly, the wind was rather cold and the ship was listed to port. Purser McElroy said that the most likely explanation was because too much coal was being used on the starboard side. This was because of a recently discovered fire onboard in Boiler Room 6. Fireman tried desperately to put it out. The fire had been caused by coal left to dry out, which would cause the fine particles of coal to rub together, which would cause a spark which spontaneously combusted, the smouldering had started during the R.M.S. Titanic's sea trials almost two weeks before.

Centrally located off the forward Grand Staircase on the starboard side of the vessel, the Purser's Office consisted of a suite of offices dedicated to conducting the Ship's business affairs, especially those that affected passengers. During the journey, passengers visited the Purser to purchase tickets for the Ship's Turkish Baths, deck chairs, swimming pool, and electric baths. And those wishing to send a radio telegram to locations on shore or greetings from the R.M.S. Titanic to friends and family on passing ships would do so from this office. After payment, the written message was conveyed to the Marconi Room on the Boat Deck by way of a pneumatic tube system.

The Purser's Office also supplied tags for any unwanted baggage, which would stay in the cargo area until the Ship docked. The R.M.S. Titanic Inc "Artifact Collection" contains several unwanted baggage tags from the second-class Purser's Office, which was located on Upper or E-deck opposite the after main staircase. In addition, the White Star Line urged passengers travelling with coins, currency, securities, and jewellery to deposit them in the Ship's safe. In return they were given a claim receipt for their possessions.

On the afternoon of the 13th April, Chief Engineer, Joseph Bell, had informed Captain Smith that the fire in Boiler Room 6 had been put out and the danger was now over, but the bulkhead that formed part of the coal bunker was damaged and a stoker was sent to rub oil on it.

First class passenger Mrs Eleanor Genevieve Cassebeer wife of Mrs. Henry Arthur Cassebeer, Jr., a resident of New York City, who is one of the survivors of the ill-fated R.M.S. Titanic, boarded the R.M.S. Titanic at Cherbourg, and was rescued in lifeboat 5, she had twice given her account of her experiences aboard R.M.S. Titanic,

Her first account which was given in an interview to a reporter from the Binghamton Press, while she was making her way to Washington where she will probably be called upon to testify before the Senatorial Investigating committee. She stopped off in the town of Binghamton at the House of the Good Shepherd, to visit her mother, Mrs. L. V. Fosdick who is very ill, when seen by the Press reporter that morning; she was preparing to leave on the 11 o'clock train. A cab was waiting for her at the door to convey her to the railroad station and she told her story hurriedly while she was preparing to depart and was published in the newspaper on Monday 29th April 1912.

Her story of the happenings of the fatal night, given exclusively to the Binghamton Press was as follows:

"My being aboard the R.M.S. Titanic was merely a matter of chance. I was visiting in Paris and being desirous of coming to America, I took the first available steamer, which, as luck would have it, happened

to be the R.M.S. Titanic, I have travelled considerably and this was the 10th time that I have crossed the Atlantic Ocean. My cabin was situated on D deck on the starboard side of the boat, and I felt the full impact of the iceberg when we struck it.

I was reclining on a couch in my room at the time and I had summoned a stewardess to inquire if it would be safe for me to allow the electric grate to burn throughout the night. She assured me that it would and immediately after she had left my cabin the shock of the cabin came. It sounded as if something were grinding and tearing away the very entrails of the monster liner. I knew immediately that there was something radically wrong and slipping on a kimono and slippers, I hurried on deck where I met Harry Anderson, a fellow passenger, and together we made our way to the bow of the boat where we found a litter of small particles of ice which was torn from the iceberg by force of the impact. We could see the berg towering some 75 to 100 feet out of the sea, and, as I afterwards learned only one-fifth of the iceberg shows above the water you can imagine the enormous size of that mountain of ice. Here we also met Thomas Andrews, who, I understand was the designer of the R.M.S. Titanic. In answer to many questions he assured everybody that we were absolutely safe and that the R.M.S. Titanic was absolutely unsinkable. He said that she could break in three separate and distinct parts and that each part would stay afloat indefinitely.

It was not long after this, however, that the pursers started to go among the passengers ordering them to go below and put on warm clothing and be prepared to embark in the lifeboats. I hurried below and dressed and when I came on deck again I found that the deck had started to list in a very alarming manner. I had already donned a life preserver which I found with some difficulty, and when I reached the deck I met Mr. Andrews again and he took me by the arm and led me to the lifeboat.

I could not hear just what he said to me at the time on account of the din, but I saw him motion to me to get into the boat, which was about to be swung over the rail 90 feet above the water. I asked him why he did not get in also, and he said: 'No, women and children first.'

Right here I wish to say that Bruce Ismay was there also, helping to load the women and children into the boat. He was dressed in pyjamas in slippers with a coat thrown over his shoulders and as the boat I was in was the sixth to leave the ship, you can see that the reports that, he (Mr Bruce Ismay) was in one of the first boats are absolutely false.

There was absolutely no panic. The discipline was excellent. I was in the boat commanded by Third Officer H. J. Pitman. There were 37 people in the boat, five of them being seamen. The boat could not hold any more at the time, as it would have been foolhardy to attempt to overload it, inasmuch as it would have buckled and broken in two from the extra weight the moment it was swung from the davits.

We saw the R.M.S. Titanic when it made its final plunge. The lights were burning until the very last moment and it was a spectacular as well as awesome sight. After the R.M.S. Titanic had sunk there were thousands of people struggling in the water crying piteously for help. Three times Officer Pitman ordered his men to turn about so that he could pick up some of them, but each time they were prevented from doing so by some of the passengers in the lifeboat who called upon the seamen frantically to go ahead and when they grasped the oars and interfered with the proper handling of the boat so that the seamen were finally forced to give up their efforts of turning back to rescue any of the unfortunates.

We were all wrapped warmly in rugs which the stewards and pursers had pinned about our waists before we got into the boat. When we were picked up by the Carpathia we were treated beautifully by both officers and the passengers. Many of whom gave up their quarters for our accommodation.

Aboard the R.M.S. Titanic I sat at the same table with Dr. O'Loughlin, the ship's surgeon and Thomas Andrews of the Holland and Wolf [sic] Building Company, I believe the name of the firm is. Mr. Andrews is said to have designed the R.M.S. Titanic. Harry Anderson was also a member of our party.

When the boat first started to list so alarmingly I immediately started to make my way to where the men were assembled because I knew that there I would assuredly be safe. I am a staunch admirer in American and British manhood.

A fact that is not generally known is that it was very hard for the men to coax the women into the lifeboats and it became necessary for some of them men to get into the lifeboats first before the women would venture into them, so confident were they that the big steamship was absolutely unsinkable. Then again some of the women absolutely refused to leave their husband's sides and it almost became necessary for Mr. Ismay and Mr. Andrews to use force in making some of the men get into the boats with the womenfolk so that they might be saved.

Another thing that is not generally known is that the R.M.S. Titanic was not ready to sail at the time she did. Mr. Andrews told me himself and said that the only reason they allowed her to go when they did was that the sailing date had already been fixed and they just simply had to start. While the ship was fitted up most sumptuously once could not help but notice that she was not prepared to sail.

There were none of the usual printed notices in the cabins. The frames for them were on the walls, but the notices themselves were not there and when I tried to find a life preserver I did not know where to look for it and was compelled to inquire of some stewards who showed me where to find it.

While I knew matters were very serious I did not realize just how badly we were off until I came up on deck the last time and stumbled over the ropes with which they were preparing to lower the lifeboats. My boat was the third to leave the starboard side and the sixth to leave the ship".

The second was in the form of a letter to her son in 1932, some 20 years after the disaster, with the help from all the notes that she had made at the time, while being rescued aboard the Carpathia, describing her voyage on the R.M.S. Titanic, below her accounts of that incredible voyage.

May 1932

My Son,

I had thought, before my memory fails me, to give to you this account of my experiences on board the R.M.S. Titanic, for I think it is my duty to make sure no one in our family forgets the story of this ship. In 1912, my former idea was to send a complete manuscript of my adventures to the commission which role was to shed light on the sinking, but Mr. Cassebeer made me change my mind. I think that at the time he preferred me not to take part in this. So what you're holding in your hands is my first and only account of the tragedy, which took place already twenty years ago. Can you believe it?

The maiden voyage of the R.M.S. Titanic has remained fresh in my memory, though. But, I have to confess, I did have to refer to the notes I had taken on the "Carpathia" to write the present document.

The R.M.S. Titanic was simply superb; a real marvel and a feast for the eyes. Luxury and refinement prevailed. I had never witnessed such a remarkable spirit of comradeship on a ship before. Everyone seemed to be in a good mood. The weather to, I have to mention it, was particularly comfortable for the month of April. I got on the R.M.S. Titanic at Cherbourg, in the north of France. I had decided to return to New York sooner, on account of the delicate health of Mr. Cassebeer, which I had been warned of only a week before sailing. While I was getting on board our ship, a young woman, embarked in England, was bidding farewell to her parents, who were getting ready to leave the R.M.S. Titanic. I later learned that this bright young woman was in fact an Irish countess, whose parents travelled with her as far as Cherbourg. I do not think that at the time of this parting, these people really knew how lucky they were to leave the R.M.S. Titanic.

The entrance of the ship opened on a large and beautiful hall, where dozens of butlers were welcoming the new passengers on board, as well as directing them to their respective staterooms. My room was located on the reception deck which we used to call deck "D" and, to give you an idea of the size of this mighty ship, let's just say that there were at least four decks above my room, and four others below! We had to our disposal gymnastic rooms, tennis rooms, two large restaurants, endless promenade decks, lounges and even a pool! All of the ship's decks were, of course, connected with electric elevators. The first days of the trip were devoted to meeting passengers, unpacking luggage and chatting over cups of tea. I got used very quickly to our ship, although every day brought new surprises. I met on board a gentleman, elegant and discreet, whose name was Anderson. We had been assigned to the same table in the saloon and quickly got along very well. I often played card games with him and a lady from Los Angeles in the music room (a very large, all-green lounge with a chandelier that was magnificent).

On Sunday morning (April 14) we assisted to a religious ceremony in the restaurant, which was presided over by our dear captain, a tall man, very polite, who sported a white beard. It was easy to say, by giving him a single look, that his life had been entirely devoted to the sea. In the afternoon Mr. Anderson came to my stateroom (his was under mine) and asked me if I wouldn't mind taking a walk with him on deck. I told him that it was an excellent idea and that I would join him on deck as soon as I was ready. It was only when we stepped outside that we realized how much the temperature had dropped, and it was with a certain detachment that I told him there must be an ice field nearby.

This evening's dinner was perfect in every aspect. I had put on my most beautiful dress (the white muslin one that your father liked so much) and my pearl necklace from Geneva. I was dining at the purser's table, Mr. McRoy [sic] and, other than Mr. Anderson, my table companions were: to my left the journalist Stead and a Mr. Steward [sic], and to my right Mr. Smart, who was always smiling, as well as a small family (a mother and two children) whose name was Crompton [sic]. Mr. Stead and Mr. Steward were entertaining me with fantastic stories from ancient fairy tales, while Mr. Anderson and I were sharing memories from our respective trips throughout Europe. The Cromptons were most discreet and only very rarely joined our conversations, although I do not wish it to be understood that I found them to be of bad company. Mrs. Crompton's children were impeccably educated, and the mother herself was always of extreme courtesy. Every evening, at dinner time, Mrs. Crompton paused before me to compliment my attire, a small attention that I found particularly touching.

After dinner, in the huge hall which I have already described, we assisted to a concert given by the "R.M.S. Titanic's orchestra which, like every other night, was divine. Then, at around eleven o'clock, I felt ready to retire. I bid good night to my comrades, and Mr. Anderson escorted me to my room, which was icy cold due to a porthole that had been left open. I closed it and turned on the electric heater. I had already prepared for the night and was brushing my hair before the mirror when I felt a slight vibration, and then I heard a long howl, just as if the R.M.S. Titanic was crying in pain. My wrist-watch indicated 11:44, and I am convinced that this is the exact hour of the collision, as purser McRoy himself, after dinner, had adjusted my watch to ship's time. It is when the engines stopped that I started to be panicked, so I immediately decided to dress. I was just finishing lacing my boots when Mr. Anderson came to knock at my door. He was wearing a lifebelt and the first thing he said was that the mailroom was flooded, and that we should go to the top deck at once. But before we did so, my friend was adamant in making me wear a lifebelt. We had great trouble in finding the lifebelts, though, and we had to ask a passing steward to help us. He finally found them under my bed.

The elevators being condemned, we had to mount the steps to the top deck. At the purser's office level we bumped into Mr. Andrews, the ship's designer, whom I knew well. He seemed to be extremely busy and when he passed us he didn't even say a word to me . . . Some minutes later Mr. Anderson and I were finally outside, on the starboard side, near the boats. It was so cold outside that we had to take shelter into the gymnastics room. Mrs. Astor, the wife of the millionaire, was already there and was so tired that she constantly had to put her head to her husband's chest in order not to fall asleep and fall to the floor! I was admiring the different machines in the room when an officer blew his whistle on deck. So we got back outside to listen to the orders. Two officers were supervising the loading of the boats. The first was tall and young and the second was short and was sporting a moustache. Both of them were waving to the women to step into the boats, but few of them were willing to take that risk, so a few men had to get in first before the women could follow. Mr. Ismay was *there, and constantly repeating the officer's orders as soon as they were given, which gave way to an argument between the two men.*

The loading of the boats was very quickly carried. Mr. Anderson helped me get in the boat, but he himself did not step in. Until I saw him again safe and sound on the "Carpathia", I feared for my friend's safety and prayed that he was not on the ship when it took its final plunge. So it was with great relief that I came upon him in one of the lounges of our savoir-ship. I believe that you are well aware of the end of that story, from the disappearance of the R.M.S. Titanic to our arrival at the Cunard's pier, so I won't bother describing again to you the details of that chapter. Before I end this letter, I want to express my gratitude to the ship's crew, to their courtesy, and to the perfection of their services during that fateful night. The officers and stewards showed great courage and, without them, everybody on board would have drowned. So I thank them all before God.

Geneviève Cassebeer

On Sunday 14th April was one of the most famous dinner parties to have taken place in the À la carte restaurant, given in honour of Captain Edward J. Smith, who would sit at the head of the table, this party was hosted by George and Eleanor Widener from Philadelphia, (this party was re-created in the 1958 movie "A Night to Remember"). Two other prominent Philadelphia couples were invited to join the Wideners that evening, the Thayer's and the Carters, like George Widener, John B. Thayer had inherited most of his wealth, but also worked his way up from clerk to 2nd vice president of the Pennsylvania Railroad. Although William E. Carter's income derived from his father who acquired coal mines, his social life had been enhanced by his marriage to Lucille Polk, who's descended from a relative of James Knox Polk, the 11th President of the United States.

Joining these grandees of Philadelphia society were two of the R.M.S. Titanic's most sought-after table companions, Captain Edward J. Smith, the ship's urbane and popular commanding officer, and Major Archibald Butt, the ship's most famous bachelor, who was a friend and military aide to William Howard Taft, the President of the United States, Captain Smith excused himself from the party around 8 p.m. to make his way to the bridge, he discussed the weather and how calm the sea was with Second Officer Lightoller. Then at 9.20 p.m. Capt. Smith retires to his cabin, for the night leaving word that he should be called "if anything becomes the least doubtful".

Apart from Bruce Ismay and Captain Smith, the only other Officer who regularly dined with the passengers was the Chief Purser; approaching what Hugh McElroy always classed as his retirement from sea duties (he had always set his sights on becoming Passenger Manager for White Star, similar position to that of his Father-in-Law). The Titanic's First Class Restaurant had tables that were designated to certain people from the White Star they were Bruce Ismay he had a two-seater table but preferred to dine alone, Captain Smith and Chief Purser McElroy who both had eight seated tables within the First Class Restaurant.

The Liverpool "Journal of Commerce" of the 8th May 1912, contained the following notice: "It has been said that so pronounced was the popularity of Mr H. W. McElroy, the R.M.S. Titanic's Chief Purser, that many people who frequently crossed the Atlantic, timed their voyage so as to sail on the same ship with him, and would go to some extraordinary lengths to be seated on his table with him. They thought of him as the Commodore Purser of the Line.

Hugh seems to have been almost as popular as Captain Smith. His strong sense of humour was so popular with the passengers that they often timed their journeys with him in mind, many a times Hugh had held his own with a difficult passenger without giving cause for offence. The Chief Steward was responsible for all seating arrangements within the 1st Class Restaurant, although Hugh had the final say on all arrangements that the Chief Steward made, although very rarely changed any decision, Hugh's dinner companions were only ever altered twice during any Atlantic crossing, passengers who were assigned a seat at Purser McElroy's table, were passengers who usually dined alone, the Purser would usually invite two passengers to join him and who ever his regular diners were that evening, some of the passengers that were invited were Mr Arthur Gee, Mr William Harrison, Mr Frederic Seward, Mr Lawrence Beesley, Mr William Stead and Mrs Geneveive Cassebeer, Hugh was well known to be genial at the table, but many a times he had held his own with a difficult passenger without giving cause for offence.

The placement of the dinner companions for Hugh's last dinner aboard the R.M.S. Titanic on Sunday April 14th 1912, sitting from his left was Miss Sara Rebecca Crompton, next to her was Mr Alexander Taylor Crompton Jr who was sitting next to his mother Mrs Crompton from Lakewood New Jersey, who was sitting next to Mr John Montgomery Smart of New York he was sitting next to another New Yorker Mr Harry Anderson, then came Mrs Geneviève Cassebeer who was also a New Yorker and to her left was Mr William Thomas Stead from Westminster in London and the last dinner companions, who was sitting to the right of Hugh was Mr Albert A. Stewart who had homes in both Paris and New York, Hugh's last dinner in the 1st Class Restaurant was typical evening meal aboard R.M.S. Titanic.

On the fateful night of the 14th—15th April 1912, many people believe the first and second class safe's in the Purser's Office went down, full of gold and jewels. This is false. At 12:05am, most of the First Class Passengers headed to the Purser's Office to take out all their valuables and treasures they had put there, as they wanted their valuables to leave the ship with them. Dr. Washington Dodge said "The Purser's Office was surrounded by a crowd demanding their valuables which the purser and his assistant endeavouring to hand out as quickly as possible. Chief Purser Hugh McElroy told the Countess of Rothes "I'm glad you did not ask me for your jewels as some ladies have", he then closed the Purser's Office during the evacuation and advised all the women not to worry about their valuables, but to put on their lifebelt's and report to the lifeboats. Before the purser left his station, he locked the safe, so no opportunist thief would take anything. Hugh and his staff had retrieved valuables from most of the Purser's safes and were distributing valuables to their owners as the lifeboat's got filled.

In addition, the White Star Line urged passengers travelling with coins, currency, securities, and jewellery to deposit them in the Ship's safe. In return they were given a claim receipt for their possessions. On the night of the sinking, the pursers diligently removed a large number of those valuables from the safe, putting them into leather "Gladstone" handbags for evacuation in the Ship's lifeboats. The bags never made it to the boats and were strewn over the ocean floor. One of those bags was recovered by George Tulloch of the R.M.S. Titanic Inc. during their 1987 Expedition; this bag contained $65,000 in bank notes, over 300 gold sovereigns, a very large amount of jewellery and 2 gold watches. The choice of leather bags was particularly fortunate, since the chemicals used in tanning the hides afforded protection to delicate paper objects such as bank notes and business cards, which would have otherwise deteriorated when exposed.

Violet Jessop said that the purser was seen bringing a "Gladstone" bag out onto the boat deck. It got knocked over and a shower of sovereign's got splashed across the deck. The purser frantically grabbing the sovereign's to stuff back into the bag. I strongly believe the references that Chief Purser McElroy had worked hard to return valuables to evacuating passengers as much as was possible and with Violet's statement and the fact that George Tulloch found a Gladstone bag containing many of the passenger's valuables, plus 300 gold sovereigns, makes my belief valid.

When the Purser's safe was recovered in the 1987 Expedition, it contained only 7 silver coins. Some say, this was the second class Purser's safe. It is said that the "Rubayiat of Omar Khayyam" was stored in the first class safe, but after the collision, it was transported into a Gladstone bag to be taken off in a lifeboat, but when no space was found, that was secure, it was returned and placed in the first class safe, still in the bag, Hugh strongly believed it would be safer to remain in the Gladstone bag.

Samuel Rule bathroom steward was asked at the British Inquiry, "When you got up to the boat deck did you get any other order "No", as I passed up the staircase, I got to A deck and I saw Mr McElroy the Chief Purser and Mr. Dodd, the Second Steward They were in deep conversation. I thought to receive some orders from them, but there were no orders given, and I passed onto the next deck, the boat deck".

Hugh was forward where collapsible "C" had been fitted to the lifeboat davits. Two men jumped into the boat and Purser McElroy is said to of fired his gun twice into the air as First Officer Murdoch ordered them out, this account was verified by first class passenger Jack Thayer who stated at the US senate inquiry that.

It had been said "There was some disturbance in loading the last two forward starboard boats. A large crowd of men was pressing to get into them. No women were around as far as I could see. It was every man for him self. Purser McElroy, as brave and as fine a man as every lived, was standing up in the next to last boat, loading it, two men, I think they were dinning-room stewards, dropped into the boat from the deck above. As they jumped, he fired twice in the air. I do not believe they were hit, but they were quickly thrown out by Purser McElroy, he also did not take a boat and was not saved.

The conclusions were, that putting the sensationalist third hand newspaper accounts aside, there is reasonable documentation to suggest that there were several gunshots incidents, other than the warning shots admitted to, by Fifth Officer Lowe, Namely:-

(a) Warnings shots, attributed to either First Officer Murdoch or to Purser McElroy, were reported by First Class Passengers Mr. Hugh Woolner and Mr. Jack Thayer at collapsible C. These were entered into evidence during the Senate Inquiry, but not thoroughly investigated.

(b) One or more warning shots, attributed to Second Officer Lightoller, was reported by First Class Passenger Archibald Gracie at the Senate Inquiry but later retracted. This incident was not thoroughly investigated.

(c) Both First Class Passengers Mr Hugh Woolner and Mr Hokan Bjornstorm-Steffansson heard pistol shots. They were fired by Purser McElroy to prevent a rush on collapsible D, which had been fitted, into the davits, previously occupied by lifeboat 1. The men rushed over and helped the Officer pull the men out of the boat and the loading of the lifeboat soon resumed.

(d) Third class Passenger Mr Eugene Daly and First Class Passenger Mr George Rheims both wrote letters stating that they witnessed two men being shot down by a Officer at collapsible A, which was then followed by the Officers own suicide. Unfortunately both Mr Eugene Daly and Mr George Rheims were not invited to testify at either the Senate or British Inquiries, also, both were discredited as being cowards in newspaper accounts, which was the likely reason they were not invited to testify.

This of course was possible, that more gunfire incidents occurred than those described here, as James Cameron (who Directed the 1998 blockbuster movie "Titanic") surmised during a conversation with R.M.S. Titanic author Mr Charles Pellegrino, "Only one-third of the R.M.S. Titanic's people lived to tell what they saw; so as a rough estimate we must be missing two-thirds of the shooting incidents that actually occurred that night.

Purser McElroy was also seen at boat 9 where he was assisting in the loading. The Chief Officer and First Officer Murdoch was supervising, Mr Bruce Ismay was with them also, Mr Ismay was talking to Purser McElroy. I do not think there were any other officers there. Mr Widgery R.M.S. Titanic's swimming Instructor also said "I was asked by Purser McElroy "If I understood anything about lifeboats?" I said "I understood a little" and just then some biscuits came up from the storekeeper. I helped him put one of the boxes into the bottom of the boat, I was then told by Purser McElroy to get into the boat. William Ward, Saloon Steward said "Purser McElroy sent me along. They had taken the canvas off of No. 9 and lowered it, we lowered her down to the level of the boat deck, and a sailor came along with a bag and threw it in the boat. This man said he had been sent down to take charge of the boat by the captain. The boatswain's mate, Haynes, was there, and he ordered this man out of the boat, and the man got out again. He stayed there for three or four minutes, and the purser took hold of my arm and said, "Get in the boat and help the boatswain's mate pass the ladies in." So I got in the boat, and stepped on the side, and the pursers said are you all ready? Haynes answered "Yes" and we started to pass the ladies and children into the boat. We thought we had them all in, and the purser called out, "Are there any more women?"

With the water at C Deck, and rapidly rising, Purser McElroy was talking cheeringly and encouragingly to the second class Purser Reg Baker and also the Purser's assistants, they were joined by Dr. O'loughlin and also Dr. Simpson, for a brief time, afterwards they were joined by Second Officer Lightoller, he was sweating from his work at the boats and Dr. Simpson joked "Hello Lights are you warm", after spending most of the night on the starboard side of the ship, loading passengers into the lifeboats, Purser McElroy had bidden "Good-bye" to those on board, he turned to his assistants and said "Well boys, the last boat has gone. I'm afraid we must eat sand for supper to-night", the small group shook hands and said their personal goodbyes, and waited for the inevitable.

Second Officer Lightoller later said in the US inquiry "I draw the conclusion that everyone was notified, by the manner and under the circumstances under which I met them last. It was obvious to me that everything with regard to their duty had been done by the mere fact that shortly before the vessel sank I met both the pursers, Mr. McElroy and Mr. Barker also their four assistants, along with Dr. O'Loughlin, and Dr: Simpson, They were just coming from the direction of the bridge. They were evidently just keeping out of everybody's way. They were keeping away from the crowd so, as not to interfere with the loading of the boats. McElroy, if I remember, was walking around with his hands in his pockets. The purser's assistant was coming behind with the ship's bag; which to me meant that all the detail work had been attended to. I think one of them had a roll of papers under his arm, showing that they had been attending to their detail work."

Finally Purser McElroy was last seen standing on the Boat-Deck near the gymnasium, beside mail clerk Mr William Logan Gwinn, giving him words of encouragement, for what was about to happen, both men died in the sinking of the R.M.S. Titanic.

Richard (Hugh's brother), his last words regarding his brother, "Need it be added, that one who was so brave was also a true catholic." He had received Holy Communion in Southampton shortly before sailing, and Hugh's last message to his brother was, "Do not forget me in your daily Mass."

—R.M.S. Titanic Timeline—

* R.M.S. Titanic prepares to depart from Berth 44 in Southampton, England, just before noon, on Wednesday, the 10th April, 1912, the Blue Peter pennant, indicating 'Imminent Departure', was run up R.M.S. Titanic's foremast. The throaty triple-valve whistles were heard three times right across Southampton. The tugs were all in place to nudge and heave at the mass of the hull, until such time that R.M.S. Titanic's mighty engines could turn the propellers out in open water. The lines holding the enormous liner against the dock were cast off, and the five comparatively tiny tugs began their heavy work. Pushing and pulling at the massive hull, constantly in touch with each other by a series of whistles, the tugs were working hard. But once out on the River Test, upon which Southampton is built, the tugs dropped all of their lines. R.M.S. Titanic's telegraph rang out, and the mighty engines started to turn the propellers, R.M.S. Titanic is set for her maiden voyage, a six-day trip across the Atlantic to New York.

* R.M.S. Titanic arrives at Cherbourg, France, at 6.30 p.m. R.M.S. Titanic drops anchor and the Two White Star tenders, "Traffic" carrying third class passengers plus all the mail, was the first to come alongside, carrying 102 third class passengers, next to come alongside was "Normadic", she was carrying 144 first class passengers and 26 Second Class, which included among it's passengers, the Astor's, Wideners, Thayer, Spedden also Molly Brown and Mrs Geneviève Cassebeer, to name just a few, also aboard Normadic were 26 second class passengers, making a total of 272 passengers to come aboard,. R.M.S. Titanic didn't remain in Cherbourg any longer than was needed to drop off and pick up some passengers, as dinner was delayed and would be served after the ship had left the port of Cherbourg.

* Departs from Cherbourg at 9.00 p.m. sailing down the English Channel heading towards the Southern coast of Ireland.

- Thursday, April 11th 1912, arriving in Queenstown (Cobh), Southern Ireland, at 11.30 a.m., she was anchored a couple of miles offshore. Two, White Star tenders, "America" and the "Ireland", ferried the passengers, their luggage and the mail to and from the ship. Also aboard, hiding under the mailbags, was one of R.M.S. Titanic's fireman, John Coffey, whose home was listed as Queenstown on the crew's signing-on sheets. He deserted R.M.S. Titanic before she sailed and came ashore, and must have felt like the luckiest man in the world when the reports of R.M.S. Titanic's demise began to filter through only days later, another incident happened in Queenstown harbour when a soot-faced stoker climbed up inside the engine room ventilation systems, inside the dummy forth funnel to get some fresh air, and peered down on the passengers, Father Brown actually took a photo of the stern of Titanic has he departed and captured the stoker peering down, to some aboard, it was a very bad omen, symbolizing an impending doom, R.M.S. Titanic departs Queenstown at around 2:00 p.m.

- Now, with Queenstown and the Irish coast rapidly fading on the horizon, R.M.S. Titanic moved out into the open waters of the Atlantic Ocean. The crew and officers could now begin to get into their routines and watches. R.M.S. Titanic was now on her maiden voyage, across the North Atlantic.

- The weather is clear, the seas calm, on Thursday the 11th and Friday 12th April.

- On Saturday April 13th, as R.M.S. Titanic approaches the mid-Atlantic, Bruce Ismay seems determined to beat the crossing times set by "R.M.S. Titanic's" sister ship the R.M.S. Olympic, and to make New York a day early. R.M.S. Titanic increases speed to more than 22 knots.

- Sunday, April 14th dawned, and who would guess the momentous events that lay ahead? The clues kept arriving though, in the shape of Marcoigrams signal messages conveying further warnings of the ice ahead, at 9 a.m.; Cunard liner "Caronia" sent a message reporting icebergs, growlers (smaller bergs) and field ice in the area. As the morning turned to afternoon, passengers strolling outside noticed the air beginning to cool. Some people donned warmer clothing, but most preferred the interior of the vessel, to the sharp conditions outside.

- At 11:40 a.m., Dutch liner "Noordam" reports ice in much the same position as noted by "Caronia" also "Amerika" reports two large icebergs in the same area at 1:45 p.m.

- At 5 p.m., R.M.S. Titanic reaches the "corner", a navigational reference point at 42 degrees N, 47 degrees, Captain Smith delays the turn to New York, for what ever reasons we will never know, probably due to earlier ice warnings, and makes the corner 50 minutes later and 16 miles farther southwest.

- At 7:30 p.m. An ice warning from the "Californian" is intercepted.

- 8:55 p.m. Captain Smith left the party he was attending in the À la Carte restaurant and went to the bridge. He discussed the weather and how calm the sea was with Second Officer Lightoller.

- At 9:20 p.m. Capt. Smith retires to his cabin, for the night leaving word that he should be called "if it becomes the least doubtful".

- 10 p.m. R.M.S. Titanic is approaching a field of ice and bergs several miles wide.

- 11 p.m. "Californian" sends messages that it is stopped and surrounded by ice, 11:35 p.m. the "Californian's" wireless room shuts down.

- 11:40 p.m. Lookout Frederick Fleet spots a black object in their path "Iceberg dead ahead".

- 11.43 p.m. R.M.S. Titanic nightmare begins as she collides with the Iceberg.

- At 11:50 p.m. The water is already 14-feet above the keel in the first five compartments.

- 11.50 p.m. Captain Smith send out Officers to assess the damage and to report back as quickly as possible, Purser McElroy along with Captain Smith, go to the Mail Room area to assess the damage, later Hugh is seen with Mr. Dodd, the Second Class Steward, they were on A deck, and were in deep conversation about the impending evacuation.

- 12:03 a.m. Several groups go to assess the damage, on their return; Thomas Andrews makes his report to Captain Smith shortly after midnight, "R.M.S. Titanic is doomed", Captain Smith asked how long until the ship is submerged; Thomas Andrews replies, after some fast calculations, "An hour and a half. Possibly two. Not much longer." Smith ordered the boats uncovered.

- At 12:05 a.m. Smith gives the order to prepare the lifeboats, Second Officer Lightoller is in command of the starboard side, First Officer Murdoch in charge of the Port side, along with Fifth Officer Harold Lowe and Sixth Officer James Moody helping where ever they could, the order to prepare the lifeboats was overseen by Chief Officer Henry Wilde.

- At 12:10, Capt. Smith tells the wireless operators to send the distress call C.D.Q. from MGY (R.M.S. Titanic) and finally the new distress call S.O.S.

- About 12.15 a.m. Several passengers and crew see the lights of another ship; perhaps as close as 6 or 10 miles away.

- At 12:25 a.m., "Carpathia" receives distress message C.D.Q. Responses also will come from the "Ypiranga", "Frankfurt", "Baltic", and "Caronia", "Prinz Friedrich Wilhelm", "Mount Temple" and "R.M.S. Titanic's" sister ship, R.M.S. Olympic.

- 12:35 a.m. Smith gives the order to man the lifeboats and abandon ship, the evacuation has begun.

- 12:45 a.m., Joseph Boxhall fires the first of eight distresses rockets and repeats the act every five minutes.

- 12:45 a.m. lifeboat No. 7 with 28 people aboard becomes the first to get away.

- 12:45 a.m., lifeboat No. 5 with 33 people aboard.

- 12:55 a.m., lifeboat No. 3 with 32 people aboard, is lowered.

- 1:00 a.m. Second Officer Lightoller lowers lifeboat No. 8 with 28 people aboard.

- 1:05 a.m., lifeboat No. 1, with a capacity of 40 people, has only 12 people aboard.

- 1:10 a.m., Second Officer Lightoller lowers lifeboat No. 6 with 28 people aboard.

- 1:15 a.m. R.M.S. Titanic lurches to port, the deck tilting.

- 12:45 a.m., lifeboat No. 16 with 40 people aboard.

- 1.15 a.m. It was stated that Fifth Officer Harold Lowe brandishes his gun to deter men from rushing lifeboat No. 14; it finally gets away with 58 people aboard.

- 1.20 a.m. Lifeboat No. 9, The Chief Officer and First Officer Murdoch was supervising the loading, Hugh was assisting in the loading and Mr Bruce Ismay was with them also, Mr Ismay was talking to Chief Purser McElroy as the lifeboat is lowered, this time with 58 people aboard.

- 1.25 a.m. Second Officer Lightoller, lowers boat No. 12 with 30 people aboard.

- 1:25 a.m. First Officer Murdoch gets lifeboat No. 11 away with over 70 people aboard.

- 1.30 a.m. Sixth Officer James Moody lowers Lifeboats No. 13 and also lowered is No. 15, with 40 and 65 people aboard respectively. (With the rush to escape, the people aboard boat No.13 are almost crushed when it is washed under the descending boat No. 15).

- At 1:40 a.m., the mystery ship turns away or is no longer visible.

- At 1:40 a.m. lifeboat No. 10 is lowered with 35 people aboard.

- 1:45 a.m. lifeboat No. 2 is lowered with 25 people aboard.

- 1:50 a.m. lifeboat No. 4 is lowered with 32 people aboard.

- It is 2.00 a.m., Collapsible boat C had been fitted to the lifeboat davits. First Officer Murdoch commences loading, when the lifeboat is two-thirds full a group of passengers try to storm it, It was stated that Chief Purser Hugh McElroy fires his pistol twice skywards to try to attain some attention. Bruce Ismay, White Star's Managing Director, climbs aboard the boat as it is lowered with 44 people aboard, an action that will bring Bruce Ismay vilification later.

- At 2.05 a.m. Collapsible D, with 22 women and children is lowered, it was stated that Second Officer Lightoller draws his revolver to keep the men from rushing the boat. Passengers Hugh Woolner and Mauritz Hakan Bjornstrom-Steffanson make a jump for it, taking places 23 and 24 of the 47 available.

- 2.05 a.m. Capt. Smith goes to the wireless cabin and releases Phillips and Bride from duty, Phillips continues to work while Bride gather's their papers before they leave.

- At 2.15 a.m. Crewmen struggle to free Collapsible B on the roof of the officer's quarters. It will eventually float off the ship, overturned, and later saves more than a dozen men from the freezing water who balance and cling to its curved hull in the ice bound Atlantic.

- At 2.15 a.m. The last boat to leave the R.M.S. Titanic was collapsible A, also stowed on the roof of Captain Smith's quarters, becomes badly tangled in its lashings on the roof, but finally breaks free and floats away, more than 20 people climb into the swamped boat from the frozen Atlantic water, Collapsible A and B were met by a flotilla of boats, assembled by Fifth Officer Harold Lowe, who was helping to pick survivors from the sea, by the time boat A was rescued there was more than a foot of water inside, those still alive were dragged aboard Lowe's boat. The three dead were left in collapsible A, which was then abandoned to drift away into the night, when it was found a month later by White Star Liner "Oceanic", it was taken aboard and the bodies were buried at sea, whilst the battered collapsible A was taken to join the other lifeboats in New York.

- At 2:17 a.m. The last wireless signal is sent by Phillips.

- 2:17 a.m. Purser McElroy was talking cheeringly and encouragingly to his Assistant Purser Reg Baker and also to the Purser's assistants, Ernest W. King, Reginald Rice, Ashcroft and Donald Campbell, they were later joined by Dr. O'loughlin and Dr. Simpson and for a brief time by Second Officer Lightoller, they all shook hands and said their personal goodbyes, and then waited for the inevitable.

- 2:18 a.m. An increasing roar is heard by those in the boats, as everything movable in the ship breaks loose and crashes to the, by then submerged bow. The ships lights until now have been kept on only by the efforts of those heroic engineers, suddenly go out, flash once more and are then extinguished for good.

- 2:18 a.m. Purser McElroy was last seen standing on the Boat-Deck near the gymnasium, beside mail clerk Mr William Logan Gwinn, giving him words of encouragement, for what was about to happen, both men died in the sinking of the R.M.S. Titanic.

- 2.20 a.m. The bow now full of water, sinks, but is still connected by her spinal cord the keel. The stern then rises itself out of the ocean for a moment, standing proud just out of the water, loud cracking and crashing sounds are heard as she breaks her back, The stern settles back slightly, flops into the water as her bow and stern are not quite severed; with her bow now completely under water, the only thing keeping the stern afloat was the air trapped inside her, the stern then slowly raises and with a loud rumbling and the sound metal being ripped apart, the expansion joints which had held her two halves together, up until now, ripped apart, her spinal cord is finally severed, the bow plummets the 2½ miles to the ocean floor, the stern with the hissing noise of the icy waters filling the stern and trying to force the air out, her shear weight alone forces the stern to disappear beneath the freezing Atlantic Ocean, causing explosions and implosions as now the stern, plummets to the ocean floor, R.M.S. Titanic has battled against all the odds for more than two hours, but the end was inevitable, she has descended to her watery grave 2½ miles down, the bow remains almost recognisable, but the stern section, after all the explosions and implosions during her descent, caused by the air trapped inside her trying to escape, this section is almost unrecognisable as it came to rest on the sea floor.

Chapter 4

The Disaster and Aftermath

On that fateful night most of the lifeboats didn't return back to pick up any survivors, only the lifeboat of Fifth Officer Harold Lowe returned, for fear of being swamped. The screams and cries of the people in the water slowly stopped as they agonizingly died in the freezing water, mostly from Hypothermia.

"Carpathia" arrived at 4 a.m. and the first boat was picked up at 4.10 a.m. Monday April 15th, and the last of the survivors was on board by 8.30 a.m. The 16 lifeboats with which the R.M.S. Titanic was equipped were all accounted for, with the exception of collapsible A.

The Leyland Line steamer "Californian" arrived upon the scene, about 8 o'clock in the morning, the Captain of the "Carpathia" communicated with her commander, stating that all of the passengers had been rescued from the boats, but that he thought one lifeboat was still unaccounted for (which was collapsible A); and arrangements were made whereby the "Californian" made an exhaustive search in the vicinity for this missing boat, but with no avail.

R.M.S. Titanic collided with the iceberg at 11:43 p.m. on Sunday 14th April 1912. Orders were given to lower the lifeboats and muster the crew and passengers at 12:05 a.m. on Monday 15 April. The first boat was lowered at 12:45 a.m. The last boat was lowered at 2:15 a.m. The ship sunk beneath the sea at 2:20 a.m. The "Carpathia" which had raced at top speed from 58 miles away arrived at 4:10 a.m. and began picking up survivors. The "Californian" had transmitted the fact that she was stopped before the Titanic struck . . . Titanic heard that fact, as did other shipping. No crew member on the Californian ever spoke of that vessel getting going before daylight, the Californian gave her position for where she stopped. We see from the Titanic wreck position that the Californian overnight point is estimated at some 17 to 19 miles from the Titanic wreck.

After "Carpathia" arrived in New York an article appeared in The Newark Evening News on Friday, April 19th 1912 with regards to, Mrs Compton who along with her son and daughter shared Hugh's last dinner table, it tells of her accounts of that incredible night.

MRS. COMPTON TELLS OF TITANIC DISASTER

NEW YORK, April 19—Mrs. Alexander T. Compton and her daughter, Miss Alice Compton, of Lakewood, N. J., and New Orleans, two of the Titanic's rescued, reached here completely prostrated over the loss of Mrs. Compton's son Alexander, who went down with the big liner. Mr. Compton was a large stockholder in the Laurel House, Lakewood, and was also financially interested in the Waumbek, Jefferson, N. H. The family spent considerable time in Lakewood.

"When we waved good-by to my son," said Mrs. Compton, "we did not realize the great danger, but thought we were only being sent out in the boats as a precautionary measure. When Captain Smith

handed us life preservers, he said cheerily: 'They will keep you warm if you do not have to use them.'
Then the crew began clearing the boats and putting the women into them. My daughter and I were lifted
in the boat commanded by the fifth officer.

"There was a moan of agony and anguish from those in our boat when the Titanic sank, and we insisted
that the officer head back for the place where the Titanic had disappeared. We found one man with a
life preserver on him struggling in the cold water, and for a moment I thought that he was my son

There have been many accounts of a mystery ship, along with the Californian, the strongest
and most arguable I have come across is from a friend, Senan Molony, who has written many
books on the subject, "A Ship Accused" (is a must to read).

Captain Lord of the "Californian" **answered a voice tube at around 1.10 a.m., to be told of
one rocket, he says. He prescribed using Morse, to clarify the situation with regards to the
rocket and asked to be kept informed. He was only physically visited once while asleep,
at 2.05am, when told that the ship under observation had fired eight rockets and steamed
away. Lord did not recall this message, but clearly if the ship has gone away, there is little
he could do,** and informed of this, he then rolled over in an attempt to get to sleep! **(there was
a mystery ship there close to the Titanic, while the Californian's own nearby visitor was
actually a shade closer than her in a straight line to the Titanic, unseen over the SE horizon.
There may very well have been other vessels in the vicinity.)** who could of saved most, if not
all of the 1,522 passengers and crew (all those who perished in the doomed Titanic), at the
time, he shows no remorse in the deaths of all those who perished on that fateful night, it was
not until later in life that he showed remorse, furthermore, when word was finally received of
the "Titanic's" fate, the Californian pursued an odd, roundabout route to arrive there, this was
due to the fact she was given Titanic incorrect CQD position by SS Frankfurt, **and eventually
the Californian arrived around to where the Carpathia could be seen.**

My only interest in these two ships, is that the "Californian" or the "Mount Temple" may of
been close enough to saved maybe everyone aboard the R.M.S. Titanic that evening, including
Hugh, it being so, a multitude of people's lives, namely the families, would then not have
been placed in the position to have to go through such terrible traumas, of going through the
bereavement, no income, going through the hardship, of not having a man or father around
and I'm sure there are many, many other reasons.

Another ship that occasionally is put forward in the "Conspiracy Theories" as the R.M.S.
Titanic's mystery ship is the Mount Temple, the same ship which saw the Californian at 6:00
a.m. The allegations are based on the hearsay story of Dr. Quitzrau, a passenger on the Mount
Temple on the night in question. He wrote in affidavit that he overheard the ship's officers
saying they saw green rockets sometime around 3:30 a.m., while they were approaching the
R.M.S. Titanic's distress position from the west. Neither of the Inquiries, it is alleged, followed
up on the story because they had already got their man: Captain Lord, of the Californian.

In fact, the British Inquiry did conduct a search for other steamers and ships reported to be in
the area, but they only looked for a vessel resembling a small black steamer cited by Captain
Moore, and in the end they had this to say about the Mount Temple, and the reason for not
pursuing the matter further:

"As regards the Captain of the Mt. Temple, those on board must have known full well, what evidence he and his Marconi operator gave in America, and must have guessed that he and the Marconi operator would be called again as witnesses at the R.M.S. Titanic Inquiry in England and if there were any allegations which persons on board desired to make against the Captain or any evidence which they thought ought to be before the Court in England they clearly ought to have volunteered to come forward as witnesses on the subject.

and furthermore,

"If there be anything in these allegations it is a matter for grave comment that those who make them have not hitherto communicated with the Board of Trade".

Dr. Quitzrau's full affidavit, which was entered into the US Inquiry record on May 9th, is as follows:

Dr. F. C. Quitzrau,
"being duly sworn, deposes and says that he was a passenger, traveling second class, on steamer Mount Temple which left Antwerp April 3, 1912; that about midnight, Sunday April 14, New York time, he was awakened by the sudden stopping of the engines; that he immediately went to the cabin, where some were already gathered, several of the stewards and passengers, who informed him that word had been received by wireless from the R.M.S.. Titanic that she had struck an iceberg and was calling for help. Orders were immediately given and the Mount Temple course changed, heading straight for the Titanic. The Titanic was sighted by some of the officers and crew; that as soon as the Titanic was seen all lights on the Mount Temple were put out and the engines stopped and the boat lay dead for about two hours; that as soon as day broke the engines were started and the Mount Temple circled the Titanic's position, the officers insisting that this be done, although the Captain had given orders that the boat proceed on its journey. While encircling the Titanic's position we sighted the Frankfurt to the northwest of us, the Birma to the south, speaking to both of these by wireless, the latter asking if we were in distress; that about 6 o'clock we saw the Carpathia, from which we had previously received a message that the Titanic had gone down; that about 8:30am the Carpathia wirelesses that it had picked up 20 lifeboats and about 720 passengers all told, and that there was no need for the Mount Temple to stand by, as the remainder of those who were not on board were drowned."

Dr. F. C. Quitzrau
Subscribed and sworn to before me this 29th day of April, 1912.
William James Elliott:
Notary Public for the Province of Ontario [US 1098]

A few points to observe:

- Dr. Quitzrau's affidavit is hearsay—he has seen no lights himself.

- Three o'clock New York time—when they supposedly saw the R.M.S. Titanic—would be at least 4:50 a.m. R.M.S. Titanic time, if we use Bride's estimate that he was an hour and fifty minutes ahead of New York. This means that whatever lights the officers and crew of the Mount Temple saw, they could not have been the R.M.S. Titanic's—she had sank.

- Nevertheless, is it a true story that he tells? We must look to evidence from officers or crew of the Mount Temple to answer that. In the mid-summer of 1912, W. H. Baker, the new Fourth Officer on the Mount Temple, wrote to Captain Lord.

Empress of Britain,
Quebec,
August 6th 1912.

Dear Lord,

You will be surprised to get a letter from me after all these years, but when I mention the old "Conway" you will then remember me. My wife had heard that you were living quite close to us in Liscard and sent me your address, so I am writing to tell you how deeply sorry I am for you with regard to the R.M.S. Titanic affair, for I know how you must have suffered. I came home in the "Mount Temple", from Halifax that voyage, having been taken out of the "Empress" at ten minutes notice to fill up a vacancy as one of her officers had been given a shore billet on her arrival at Halifax, homeward bound. The officers and others told me what they had seen on the eventful night when the R.M.S. Titanic went down, and from what they said they were from ten to fourteen miles from her when they saw her signals. I gather from what was told me that the Captain seemed afraid to go though the ice, although it was not so very thick. They told me they not only saw her deck lights, but several green lights between them and what they thought were the R.M.S. Titanic. There were two loud reports heard, which they said must have been the finale of the R.M.S. Titanic; this was some time after sighting her, I gathered the Captain said at the Inquiry at Washington, that he was forty nine miles away—but the officers state that he was not more than 14 miles off. I must tell you these men were fearfully indignant that they were not then called upon to give evidence at the time for they were greatly incensed at the Captain's behaviour in the matter. The Doctor had made all preparation, and rooms were turned into hospitals, ect. And the crew were standing ready to help on deck, watching her lights, and what they said were the green lights burnt in the boats. On our arrival at Gravesend the Captain and Marconi Operator were sent for, also the two log books, scraps, and Chief Officers. What they wanted with the scrap log I cannot understand for there was only about a line and a half written of what occurred during the four hours and quite half a page in the Chief's book, I saw that myself. These fellows must feel sorry for you knowing that you could not in the face of this have been the mystery ship. I have been residing in South Africa for some time with my wife and family and have only within the last five years returned to England, and have taken up the sea again, and have once more had to begin at the beginning—but I live in hopes of getting promotion sometime. You will of course have heard all about our collision. I hope to see you when I get back. By the way, Rostrum was also on the "Conway" with us, as you will of course remember.

Well, no more now. All news when we meet.

Wishing you a happy issue out of all your troubles, Believe me,

Sincerely yours,
(Sgn) W. H. Baker

Note again, that Mr. Baker's letter to Capt. Lord is based on hearsay—he was not on the voyage in question, but was only posted there for the return trip back to Europe from Halifax. Note also that he mentions "green lights burnt in the boats" and deck lights from "what they thought was the R.M.S. Titanic." Even if we accept Dr. Quitzrau's estimate of the time as being "about 3 o'clock New York time," it is already later than the time that Boxhall in lifeboat No. 2, was firing green flares for the Carpathia, and the Carpathia fired rockets to let the R.M.S. Titanic's survivors know that she was on the way.

Back to the Mount Temple. A certain Mr. Notley, who was Fourth Officer on the fateful voyage, might have been one of the officers who was "greatly incensed" at Capt. Moore's behavior. Baker arranged a meeting between Notley and Lord, and late in the summer of 1912, Baker, Lord and Notley met for lunch (according to Leslie Harrison). The outcome was that while Notley offered to tell Lord all he knew about the Mount Temple on the night in question, he was not willing to provide a statement to the Board of Trade.

Finally, Baker and Lord attempted to enlist the help of the Mount Temple's Dr. Bailey, and he wrote separate responses to Baker and Lord.

To Baker:
". . . What value would an unprofessional and worthless expression of details as to what occurred on the Mount Temple is in the face of what has been found? It is clearly in Captain Lord's best plan to seek his evidence from Notley at Montreal and the officers who were on the ship at the time who saw certain things and freely discussed matters together; why come to ask me, who doesn't know the blunt end, from the sharp end of a ship?"

To Lord:
"Not being a navigating officer, no information I could give would, in the circumstances, be of the slightest use to you, when all the evidence as to what occurred on the Mount Temple on the morning of the R.M.S. Titanic catastrophe are close to you in the officers of that ship and now in the service of the Canadian Pacific Railway. These might, if obtained, be of value to you."

So, in sum, piecing together all the testimony—Capt Moore on the Mount Temple, Lord and Stewart on the Californian, the hearsay affidavits and letters of Quitzrau and Baker, and the secret statements by Gibson and Stone—the following timetable outlines the events noted by all the parties concerned:

2:20a.m.
R.M.S. Titanic sinks, having fired rockets at a ship to the north; Californian has been observing a ship to the south firing rockets, now she disappears; Carpathia and Mount Temple are several miles away, out of sight.

3:20a.m.
R.M.S. Titanic has been sunk for an hour—Boxhall is burning green flares in the boats; Carpathia is arriving from the S.E., firing two rockets to reassure R.M.S. Titanic's passengers; Californian observes three more rockets, first directly south, then S.E., farther away than the earlier rockets; Mount Temple sights green lights "in the boats" and bright deck lights further away, and hears two loud reports.

4:00a.m.
Carpathia arrives at the lifeboats; On the Californian, Stewart relieves Stone, learns about rockets, sights a new ship directly to the south; "That's not the ship I saw earlier," Stone tells Stewart; Mount Temple is slowing down, approaching the icefield from the S.W., nearing the incorrect CQD position.

4:30a.m.
Carpathia is picking up the lifeboats; Capt Lord arrives on the bridge of the Californian; Stewart and Lord on the Californian now sight a yellow funnel steamer to the S.W., 8 miles away; the yellow-funneled Mount Temple is stopped at the edge of the ice field, and estimates R.M.S. Titanic's position is wrong by 8 miles.

5.30a.m.
Capt. Lord hears from the Frankfurt about the Titanic, starts for the incorrect CQD position; Lord knows only that his ship can see a vessel near the vicinity of the SOS position, which he assumes must be the Carpathia, which has already transmitted that she is picking up boats. He then heads to the incorrect SOS position but the only ship there is the Mount Temple—and he mistakes her for the Carpathia, but Capt. Moore of the Mount Temple knows Californian is crossing the icefield because he has been told about it by Californian's wireless operator Evans.

Conclusion: The Mount Temple's officers have seen both Boxhall's green flares from the lifeboats and the Carpathia's rockets as she approached the scene. The Mount Temple's arrival at the CQD position as given by Capt. Moore and this is confirmed as taking place sometime around 4:30 am and is seen by Stewart and Lord on the Californian. Capt. Moore's testimony about his actions is most likely correct: the Mount Temple could not possibly have been the mystery ship seen from the Titanic at 2:20 a.m; or earlier.

On the 6th August 1912, one W. H. Baker wrote to Captain Lord. Baker, claimed to have served on Mount Temple during her return voyage from Halifax. I have not come across any evidence that proves he DID serve on her—According to him; Mount Temple's officers told him that their ship had not been 49 miles from Titanic, as claimed by Captain Moore, but only 14 miles. From this position, they had seen ' . . . deck lights and several green lights between them, and what they thought was the Titanic.' By some strange logic, this was supposed to prove that the SS. Californian was not the infamous 'mystery ship' seen from Titanic.

By August 1912, the transcripts of both US and English inquiries were published, and Boxhall's use of green lights was public knowledge, there is no evidence that he fired them before Titanic sank. This alone makes Baker's letter suspect, we must also remember that Baker and Rostron were on the Conway and Captain Lord was never on the stationary training ship Conway, Captain Moore presented a perfectly coherent account of his rescue mission. His starting point is on his course to Cape Sable. We know he reached the vicinity of the CQD position, because he later saw the Californian and Carpathia.

The account is finally demolished, by the discovery of R.M.S. Titanic's wreck. To pass within 14 miles of it, Captain Moore would have had to be wildly off his course for Cape Sable. His starting point of 41° 25'N, 51° 14'W is on his correct course to Cape Sable from his turning point at 41° 15'N, 50° W. Baker's claim requires him to have been about 75° off course! Unless we are to decide that Captain Moore was both a liar and a blundering incompetent, if not it would make Baker's letter like Dr Quiztrau's affidavit a case was not proven against Capt. Moore.

On the 10th August 1912, Captain Lord of the Californian wrote to the Assistant Secretary of the Marine Department, to give his version of events of that faithful night, and also because of Public Opinion and Lord Mersey decision, plus the way both the US Senate and the English enquiry were commissioned, the Leyland Line, who Captain Lord worked for, reluctantly asked for Captain Lord's resignation, after 14½ years service.

10, Ormond St
Liscard
Cheshire
Aug 10th 1912

The Assistant Secretary
Marine Dept

Dear Sir,
With reference to Lord Mersey's report on the "Titanic" disaster, he states the "California" was 8 to 10 miles from the scene of the disaster, I respectfully request you will allow me as master of the "California" to give you a few facts which proves she was the distance away that I gave some 17 to 19 miles April 14th 6.30 hrs I sent my position to the "Antillian" "Titanic", this gives me 17 miles away, and you will see it was sent some hours before the disaster April 15th about 5.30 hrs gave my position to SS "Virginian" before I heard where the "Titanic" sank, that also gave me 17 miles away, as indicated by the original Marconigram used in court.

The evidence of Mr Boxhall of the "Titanic" who was watching the steamer they had in view, states she approached them between one and half hrs, the "California" was stopped from 10.30 hrs to 5.15 hrs next day.

The steamer seen from the "Californian" was plainly in view from 11.30 hrs, the one seen by the "Titanic" was not, according to her lookout men seen until 0.30 hrs Capt Rostrum of the "Carpathia" states when at the scene of the disaster, it was daylight at 4.30 hrs, I could see all around the horizon about 8 miles North of me (This was the direction the "California" was) there were two steamers, neither of them was the "California"

Had the "California" been within 10 miles from the "Titanic" she would have been in sight, at this time from the "Carpathia", as she was in the same position as when stopped at 10.30hrs the previous evening.

With regards to my own conduct on the night in question I should like to add a little more. I had taken every precaution for the safety of my own ship, and left her in charge of a responsible officer at 0.40 hrs, with instructions to call me if he wanted anything, and I lay down fully dressed at 1.15 hrs, (25 minutes after he had seen the first signal) the officer on watch reported the steamer we had in sight was in fact her leaving, In other words was steaming away, and had fired a rocket.

I did not anticipate any disaster to a vessel that had been stopped nearby for an hour, and had ignored my morse signals, and was then steaming away, I asked him was it a Co° signal, and to signal her and let me know the result, It is a matter of great regret to me that I did not go on deck myself at this time, but I didn't think it possible for any seaman to mistake a Co° signal for a distress signal, so I relieved the officer on watch.

Although further signals were seen between 1.15 hrs and 2.0 hrs I was not notified until 2.0 hrs, and then I had fallen into a sound sleep, and message was sent to me then, I was not suffiently awake to understand, and it was sufficiently understandable to anyone that I had not realised the message, by the fact that I still remained below, curiously to see a vessel punching through the ice would have taken me on deck.

The message sent to me at 2.0 hrs was I heard later, to the effect that the steamer we had in sight at 11.30 hrs, had altered her bearings from 556 to SW ½ hr (to do this she must have steamed at least 8 miles, the "Titanic" did not move after midnight) and had fired 8 rockets, and was out of sight, the question of drink has been named as the reason I could not be aroused, I don't drink, and never have done.

Further signals were seen after 2.0 hrs but the officer was so little concerned about them, that he did not think it necessary to notify me. I was called by the Chief Officer at 4.30 hrs, and in connection he referred to the rockets seen by the second officer, I immediately had the wireless operator called, heard of the disaster, and proceeded at once, punching through the field ice to the scene, and I would have done the same earlier had I understood, as I had everything to gain and nothing to lose.

There is the communication between the second officer and the apprentice while watching the vessel that they thought she was a tramp steamer, this is the opinion at the time, which is more likely the correct one.

My employers, the Leyland Line, although they are not adverse, are convinced we did not see the" Titanic", or the "Titanic" see the "Californian"; say they have the utmost confidence in me, and do not blame me in anyway, but owing to Lord Mersey's decision and public opinion caused by this reputed, they are reluctantly compelled to ask for my resignation, after 14½ years service *without a botch of any difficulties, and if I could clear myself of this charge, would willingly undermine this decision,*

If you consider there was any laxity aboard the "Californian" the night in question, I respectfully draw your attention to the information given here, which was given in evidence, which also proves was not in my past, I am told that at the inquiry I was say from witness, this I don't dispute but I have to see why I should have to put up with all this public opinion, though no fault of neglect on my part, and I respectfully request you will be able to do something to put my conduct on the night in question, in a more favourable light to my employers and the general public.

I am Sir,
Your Obedient Servant

Stanley Lord (Sig)

The best historical account ever written on the R.M.S. Titanic disaster was, "A Night to Remember" (which was written by Walter Lord (no relation), 1956, it has never been out of print since) it records many incidents and facts of the sinking; he also wrote the sequel to "A Night to Remember" which was "The Night Lives On".

The Official British statistics given were 1,522 passengers and crew "not saved", and 706 "saved". This broke down to 1,393 men, 106 women and 53 children died in the R.M.S. Titanic disaster. 672 people were lowered into the lifeboats, 706 survivors, this broke down to 299 women, 55 children, 138 male passengers and 214 crew members were picked up by the "Carpathia", therefore 34 who went into the water were saved, (some were saved but died shortly afterwards—these were not included). These figures have been contested over the years.

The figures that most researchers accept is: Passengers and Crew aboard, appears after many years of researching, to be 2208. The number of survivors, instead of being 705 as quoted in most sources, is actually 712. Using those figures it would now appear that 1,496 people lost their lives, bearing in mind that these numbers do not include the Cherbourg cross-channel passengers nor the Queenstown passengers or even Fireman John Coffey, the above figures were researched by Phil Gowan, for which all R.M.S. Titanic researchers are indebted.

June 1912, R.M.S. Titanic's last body was recovered. The remains of First-Class Saloon steward W. F. Cheverton are buried at sea by the steamer "Ilford".

The Carpathia didn't recover bodies from the sea, but according to Purser Brown of the Carpathia 4 bodies were definitely buried at sea from the Carpathia, the morning after the sinking. These were mainly people who died in the lifeboats or died on board Carpathia, William Hoyt (1st Class passenger) was taken from boat 14 and two crewmen from boat 4 William Lyons (seaman) was still alive (barely) when taken aboard the Carpathia and Sidney Siebert (steward), Abraham Harmer (crewman) whose real name was David Livshin, who died in collapsible B, (whose body was taken from collapsible B, by Lightoller) and was identified by Dr. McGhee and there was also possibly an unidentified fireman (Edward Lindell from

Collapsible A), some sources suggest more than six burials. Lawrence Beesley, for instance, gave the number as eight, including four who had died on board, will we ever know the true figure.

On May 16th 1912 an article appeared in The New York Times, with regards to the Missing collapsible "A" from the R.M.S. Titanic.

R.M.S. TITANIC LIFEBOAT FOUND AT SEA

Bodies of One passenger and two members of crew in it

A message was received last night by the agents of the White Star Line from Capt Smith of the incoming "SS. Oceanic", stating that the R.M.S. Titanic's missing collapsible boat had been picked up with the three bodies in it that were there when Third Officer Lowe took the twenty one living persons out of it, the message reads:

"May 12th, Latitude 30.56 (39.56?) North, Longitude 47.01. picked up collapsible boat containing three bodies, one apparently Thomas Beattie, passenger; one sailor, one fireman, both unidentified; also coat with letter in pocket addressed to Richard N. Williams; one cane, Duane Williams; also in the boat a ring, with the inscription "Edward and Gerda".

This boat has been adrift on the ocean since April 15, the date of the R.M.S. Titanic's loss/

Chapter 5

The bodies of Makay-Bennett

"MacKay-Bennett" left Halifax Wednesday, April 17th at 12.28 p.m. and on Friday, April 19th at 6:45pm she picked up a lifebelt with Allan Line marked on it, with still a fair way to go, then on Saturday, April 20th. 7 p.m. she passed an enormous berg about 200 feet high and some small ice evidently from large bergs, not wishing to have the same fate she stopped for the night. Still a lot of wreckage drifting about, arrived at the wreck site on Sunday, April 21st. at 6:45 a.m. it quickly became apparent that there were far more bodies floating in the ocean than anyone had expected, they lowered a boat to search for bodies, picked up first body of a Danish boy.

On Monday, April 22nd, they came across an enormous quantity of wreckage, they also came upon a lifeboat bottom up, with its side smashed in, and the lifeboat was left to its own devises to float off. They picked up quite a few bodies, the body of Col. J. J. Aster being amongst them, bodies floated very high in water in spite of the sodden clothes and things in pockets. Apparently the people had lots of time and discipline must have been splendid, for some had on their pyjamas, two and three shirts, two pairs of pants, two vests, two jackets and an overcoat. In some pockets a quantity of meat and biscuits were found, while in the pockets of most of the crew quite a lot of tobacco and matches besides keys to the various lockers and stateroom doors were found. On this day they buried 15 bodies some of them very badly smashed and bruised.

Also on that Monday a body was pulled from the sea by the crew of the "MacKay-Bennett" among the effects on the body were keys tagged "Linen locker No 1—C Deck" and the address "Miss McElroy, Layton, Spottisbury, Dorset", the letter was addressed to Miss McElroy who originally was thought to be Hugh's sister, Charlotte Mary, who at that time was the only "Miss" in the family, and who was at the time planning to live in Dorset, but Barbara's middle name is also Mary and it was later identified as she, who was living at "Layton", Spettisbury (not Spottisbury) in Dorset, Barbara had moved from the "Polygon" in Southampton to Spettisbury over a previous family argument, also Spettisbury is where St. Monica's Priory is, this is were Hugh was dismissed by order of the Abbot General Felix Menchini with the Canons Regular of the Lateran in 1891.

Body No 157 was tentatively identified by Research Group 1991. Description: male; estimated age 32; dark hair; Clothing: ship's uniform; white jacket; ship's keys; 10 pence; 50 cents; they also found his beloved fountain pen (that was given to him by his father, Richard). The body was not immediately identified as Hugh McElroy, but was listed as a "D. Lily, Steward" and someone had pencilled on the listing a notation "Probably McElroy Purser", the actual body description does not attribute a name to this body, No 157 and was still unidentified in 1912. it would remain that way for a further 79 years, then in 1991, he was recorded as Herbert? the transcribed entry for body 157, would lead one to believe that the name "Herbert W. McElroy" was written in the description, The individual who transcribed the body descriptions for Encyclopedia Titanica in 1991 appears to have taken liberties in that respect and indicated names for some bodies which were unidentified in 1912 but have since been identified. Since "Herbert" had long been thought to be McElroy's given name, that's the name the (Research Group 1991) transcriber Rob Ottmers seems to have used, the list was based on information put together at that time and was not intended to be a verbatim copy of the original list. the mistake was not made at the coroners court in Halifax as we were originally lead to believe, when his effects were checked and identified by Mr Percy Mitchell who signed a declaration and certified that the deceased person was possibly a Steward or Officer of the R.M.S. Titanic as he was dressed wearing a white officer's dinner jacket, when he was found, they investigated but never put a name to the body, the pencilled notation on the listing, was totally missed and it was not until 1991 that they found out who he was, but because of the mistake made in 1991, giving him the name of "Herbert", this would in a way, haunt Hugh right up to the present day, a thing I have given up trying to rectify, on the many web sites on the internet.

My personal thanks to both Chris Dohany & Rob Ottmers of the Research Group 1991, your apologises are accepted, by the way his given "nick" name was Mac, same as mine, not Herbert.

Unidentified, Male Age 32 Dark hair Hugh McElroy Purser	157	Buried at sea.	Ship's uniform, white jacket. Key tagged linen locker, No.1 C Deck. Address found in effects: Miss McElroy, Layton, Spottisbury, Dorset. 10 pence; 50 cents Fountain pen

Because his condition was decomposed, beyond preservation it was decided by Captain F. H. Larder of the "MacKay-Bennett" that he should be buried at sea, so at 8 p.m. on Monday 22nd of April 1912, Hugh was committed to the sea as one of 15 who were buried that day. The service was conducted by Canon Kenneth C. Hind who was from All Saints Cathedral in Halifax, Nova Scotia and was aboard to perform such duties. Upon reaching the wreck site, "MacKay-Bennett" found it was quite apparent that there were so many bodies in the ocean, more than anyone had anticipated. It did not take long before her crew ran out of embalming supplies, she received new supplies from the "SS Sardinian" of the Allan Line, "MacKay-Bennett" had to bury many of the victims at sea as regulations only allowed embalmed bodies to be brought ashore in America, not surprisingly, given the class attitudes of the period, that the bodies of third class and crew members that were chosen to be buried at sea, along with all the other badly damaged bodies.

It seems strange that most people aboard R.M.S. Titanic had some sort of premonitions about sailing on the R.M.S. Titanic, Dr. O'loughlin, Violet Jessop, and Eugene Daly at least a good portion of the crew and passenger while anchored In Queenstown harbour, a soot-faced stoker climbed up inside the dummy forth funnel to get some fresh air, and peered down on the passengers, to some onboard, it was a bad omen, symbolizing an impending doom. I'm certain there are others, all have to be documented somewhere with regards to their premonitions. Purser McElroy had suffocating nightmares, but is it a coincidence, that according to Dr. Beaumont of the R.M.S. Olympic who said, "Purser McElroy had been woken on several occasions on the R.M.S. Olympic due to suffocating nightmares, which gave way to him having some premonitions about sailing on the R.M.S. Titanic, he would have nightmares of being in a dark tunnel or cave with no means of escape".

There were several strange coincidences that had connections to Chief Purser Hugh McElroy

➤ That when the "MacKay-Bennett" set's sail on the 17th April 1912, to pick up the bodies from the R.M.S. Titanic, on her second day out (19th April) at 6.45 a.m. she picked up a lifebelt with the Allan Line markings on it, she did not reach the wreck site for another day and half, arriving on 21st April 1912. Mr. John Ennis, Hugh's father-in-law was formerly Passenger Manager of the Allan Line; it was also the shipping line which Hugh had initially started his sea faring career as ship's purser.

➤ That the "MacKay-Bennett" received new supplies from the "SS Sardinian" again a ship from the Allan Line.

On hearing of the disaster, Hugh's brother, Reverend the Prior Richard McElroy RCL travelled from Bodmin up to Southampton, he was accompanied by Abbott Aloysius Smith a fellow-priest who was also at St Mary's Priory, Bodmin in Cornwall (they first met at Cotton Hall College and became lifelong friends), Abbott Aloysius Smith's brother Reginald George Smith was coincidentally a saloon steward on the R.M.S. Titanic and had also perished, in the disaster.

A letter was part-published in May 1912 in the "Northern Constitution", a newspaper based in Coleraine, Northern Ireland, and was republished in an article by reporter/historian Senan Molony in the White Star Journal, quarterly organ of the Irish R.M.S. Titanic Historical Society, in September 2002. The letter was written by a man named Smith, manager of a club for serving merchant mariners in New York, to his brother Hugh Smith who lived in Main Street, Portrush, Co Antrim, in late April 1912, part of which read. "Mr McIlroy, the purser, had quite a sum of money for me, but I'd give a great deal more to see his genial smile again. He was a fine big-hearted Galway man, and a prince to boot. Mr Lightoller told me that the last time he spoke to Mac, he said: Well, it looks as if we will have sand for supper tonight, I don't think he (McElroy) got down so far, for he was a clean big fellow".

In September 1915, Senator LaFollette of Wisconsin who was also a good friend of President Roosevelt gave his name to the act that would determine the number of lifeboats necessary for the safety for the passengers. "The LaFollette's Seaman's Act of 1915" came into force which stipulated that the number of passengers on a ship, not the gross tonnage would determine its lifeboat capacity.

Chapter 6

The life and Friends of my Nan

It could be said that some people have the luck of a cat with nine lives; one of them has to be Violet Constance Jessop, who along with my Nan, started to guide my inspiration to find the true facts on my Great Uncle Hugh.

Violet who was born 2nd October 1887, had an adventurous streak in her life, she joined the White Star Line as a stewardess, (it could be said that she was following the steps of her mother, who was also a stewardess) Violet had a unique claims to fame, that along with John Priest (fireman), they were aboard all three of the White Star's Olympic-class ships when they came to grief, they were both working on board the "R.M.S. Olympic" when it had a costly collision with "H.M.S. Hawke" in 1911, and six months later survived the last, ghastly hours of the "R.M.S. Titanic", I know Violet shared a stewardess's cabin on "C" deck with Elizabeth Leather, who was also from the Bedford Park area in London.

To cap everything Violet along with John Priest, were both on board the "H.M.H.S. Britannic" in 1916 when it hit a mine in WW1 and sank in 55 minutes, while cruising off the Island of Kea, in the Aegean Sea and went straight to the bottom. Violet's lifeboat was sucked into the still turning propellers, her injuries included a skull fracture that she did not discover for many years.

My first encounter with this fine lady was in 1962, I had just bought my first car a "newish, 6 months old" Ford Popular, for a massive total of £150.00, (of which most was borrowed, from my Dad), and on my first motoring holiday with my sister and my Nan, in Great Yarmouth, Norfolk. I remember we went to meet a few old friends of my Nan's, one in particular, (I learned from my Mum, was Violet) we were invited to her home for tea, it was 1963, just a year before my Nan died, she must of known she didn't have long, as she wanted to meet all her old friends, that she had not seen for many years. Violet was an elderly lady, I recall, she had been a friend of my Nan's for a long time, they had barely seen each other since Nan had moved from Flander Road, Bedford Park, in London, to Dorset, but they had corresponded and kept in touch with one another.

I must of been about 20 years old at the time of our motoring holiday, we travelled down from Liverpool to my Nan's house in Dorset,, the next day we travelled to Great Yarmouth in Norfolk to a little country Guesthouse, Nan decided that after a day of rest, we would have a day out and drive round the area to see some of her old friends, we had a few stops on route, along all those narrow little country lanes, when we finally called in to see one of her friends, I can still remember their discussions (That's what they called it—gossiping is what I call it?), at such a young age, I always remember that moment because of her big garden with those funny looking chickens, with fluffy feet (strange how some memories stick in your mind) but mostly because she called my Nan "Bessie" which up to that point, I only thought was used by our family, I digress, two elderly ladies happy to be talking about the past with a little bit of juicy gossip thrown in, so much to talk about, so little time to do it in, it was one of those moments that my Nan, looked so happy, perhaps that's also why that sticks in my mind.

She would go on about how hard life was without hardly any money in those days; Violet was very briefly married to her Ned. He was an old bachelor in his mid forties at the time of their marriage, I think he lived somewhere in or around Southampton, I think he also had something to do with the merchant navy, it may have been in engineering, Her father-in-law was also a Master Mariner and her mother was also a stewardess, so seafaring appears to have been in the blood of all involved. They married in a Catholic ceremony, but that did not prevent a divorce after about a year later, there were no children, and after he died she spent the rest of her life alone, because Ned would always remain her number one love, and just like my Nan, after Grand pops died would revert back to her maiden name, I myself think it was because they were both Catholic and had come to terms with life, they had both lost the one thing in life that meant anything to them and were prepared to spend the rest of their lives with it's memory.

I think the reason they got on so well, was because Violet had a Covent Education, Just like my Nan, and had also held the position of a governess, to a family with children. I know she had a love for Liverpool and its docks, why the docks, I don't know.

When on the subject of Hugh, both my Nan and Violet would say, "that I would get to know my Great Uncle one day and that I should be proud of him" also Violet would comment, that "He was always the most well mannered and highly respectable man, in fact the finest man she ever met", the fondest memory I have of Violet now is, apart from her strictness, was, when the time came to say our goodbyes, she would kiss both my sister and me on both cheeks, (at the time I hated it, I always thought that was French kissing, possibly because I was too young to know any better) Violet would turn to my Nan and remark "doesn't he have the look of Hugh?" Thinking back, they must have met, Hugh and Violet, after all, they both had their cabin accommodation on the same deck "C" Deck., also they both had seafaring running into their respective families.

I discovered, during my research, that Hugh admired Violet very much; she would always suppress large tragic events and magnify romantically low key events. The life of a maid was very hard and poorly paid and most sacrificed their home and family life for the rigid task masters of the cruise liners as they span the world's oceans in toil and labour, she was a handsome, practical, intelligent and a very caring woman. I very much liked her character and she weaves a saga of another age, an age I can easily relate to, even by today's standards.

Violet treasured those secret memories up to 1963 and beyond, after all she had spent more than 42 hard years at sea, before retiring to her lovely country thatched cottage in Wetherden, Great Ashfield, a few miles outside Bury St Edmunds in Suffolk, where she died of congestive heart failure on Wednesday 5th May 1971 aged 84, and is buried in Hartest Hill Churchyard, (Hartest is a village near Long Melford in Suffolk) her sister still lives in the village, that was possibly why she chose to be buried there and in 2007 her sister and her niece replaced the 3 family graves with new headstones, I often go there just to pay my respects, on my way to Long Melford where I use to run my business, and afterwards call in to see old friends in Sudbury and Bury St Edmunds,, just to have a pint and a chat, about the old days?? (Not to gossip, you understand?).

The American author, John Maxtone-Graham who published Violet's book in 1997, called "R.M.S. Titanic Survivor, the memoirs of Violet Jessop, Stewardess", visited her at her cottage in Great Ashfield in 1970 the year before she died. Violet's personal diary was entrusted to her niece Mrs Margaret Meehan, who was very close to Violet in those later days, and still lives in the village of Great Ashfield.

The one thing I always wondered about, considering that Hugh and Barbara had been "long-time sweethearts" sadly they had such a short time together, from Hugh and Barbara's marriage on the 9th July 1910, to Barbara's remarriage a period of only 3 years, why the sudden change? So close after Hugh's death, was it the money £4330.13. 3d, (which converted into today's money, would be, a considerable large sum if adjusted for inflation, just over a £1 million.) "No", this was not the reason; the Ennis family had and were use to money.

After the R.M.S. Titanic disaster, Barbara desperately needed some space, so she decided to returned home to be with her ailing Father, Barbara's house "Layton" in Spettisbury in Dorset, was finally sold to her Sister-in-Law Charlotte, for a sum of £450, after the intervention of Charlotte's new husband, a truce was finally agreed between Charlotte and Barbara, with regards to a previous family arguments.

Barbara went back to Ireland to be with her father, who was by then was very ill, and on October 18th 1913 he died, Barbara returned to Toxteth, Liverpool and on February 1914 quite suddenly got remarried to a Mr George C. Booker, they both moved back to Ireland and in a period covering just over two years she gave birth to a girl and two boys (twins), one of the boys moved to Nottingham, while Barbara's remaining family stayed in Ireland, I met Colin, who is Barbara's grandson on my last visit to Ireland in 2007 and still regally keep in touch by email. I can sympathise and understand Barbara's position at that time, getting remarried as soon as possible, because her child bearing years were disappearing very quickly, and in those days a married woman who was not bearing children, was a very taboo subject, and was even frowned upon by the Catholic Church both in England and more so in Ireland at that time.

On July 1913, Charlotte, was living at Flander Road, Bedford Park, Chiswick in London after a massive argument with both her mother (Jessie) and Barbara, to have her name removed from the dependants list of the R.M.S. Titanic Relief Fund, because she was about to give up the Roman Catholic church to become a Protestant (Church of England), the reason was to married the man she loved (who's religion was Protestant), but the marriage lasted just three years, because he suffered a massive heart attack and died in 1918, Charlotte reverted back to her maiden name of McElroy, for whatever her reasons, but she was caring for herself and her two young children, Charlotte realised the enormity of what she had done, in changing her religion and prepared herself for the onslaught, given that her family were for generations staunch Roman Catholic's, she would be excommunicated from the family as well as the church, and because the Roman Catholic church felt she had committed such a grave offence against the ecclesiastical authorities, the Bishop would put her under interdict (denying her confession, communion or consecrated burial), which made it a mortal sin for a Catholic to support her.

The note (described as "the address"), that they found on Hugh, must have been the last thing he wrote, to his beloved wife Barbara, which must have been scribbled quickly, given the time facture, Hugh wanted to make amen's, for any upset he may of caused Barbara, re: regarding a suggested move to his beloved Cornwall, where as Barbara wanted to move back to her father's house in Ireland, due to the fact of his health was failing, after all, this was suppose to be Hugh's last trip, then he wanted to retire from the sea, as he had set his sights on becoming the Passenger Manager for the White Star Line.

Barbara in turn sent the note (described as "the address"), to the family, to be placed in his coffin before the burial, along with all his other belongings which was forwarded by White Star, with the exception of his fountain pen, which still remains in our family,

Chapter 7

Epilogue

Over the year's I have tried to get the answers to the many, many questions that I have been asked, myself, I have badgered my Mum with questions and all she would say is; "That's a private matter, leave it be"? My Nan died in 1964 and my Mum in 1986, I miss them both tremendously, my Nan for the way she would listen to all our problems, and the way she helped me with things most teenager goes through, and my Mum for all the things I wanted to tell and finally didn't have time to, I love and miss you both, I have kept my promise to both of them, in doing this research, the world can now know and hopefully understand Hugh, also I hope all those questions that have been asked over the years have now possibly been answered also if others wish to go further into speculation, like they have in the past, will find that there is no substitute for the truth, I hope that they will do their research rationally in locating the raw truth and with some regard to the simple fact that there are no villains in this story: just human beings with human characteristics.

The loss of the R.M.S. Titanic created a debate that has raged ever since, and probably will do so for ever, It happened in 1912, prior to two world wars, long before television, indeed, long before talking pictures. It was an era as different to today as you can imagine. There were many more crowned heads of Europe then, and servants lived downstairs in every town, and children were dressed like mini versions of their elders and told to be quite (and even more astonishing, they generally did). It was a world quite unlike our present days in nearly every respect, yet this event has even the most modern child's attention when it is spoken of. It is a story and the effects of its happening endure, and will always endure, so long as humans remain human.

While the family are truly satisfied with these events in Hugh's life, and while it does not purport to answer all the questions about Hugh, his family and the world around him, which have been raised, it does, I hope, attempt to distinguish the essential circumstances and sets out, reasoned and realistic interpretations, now the people, can now make their own judgement.

Most of the research done by myself was obtained first hand, by visiting the many places connected with Hugh; at this point I would like to say.

"Thank You" to the people I have met, who took the time and effort to supply me with items, photos and information.

"Thank You" to all those people who pointed me in the right direction, I will always be in your debt for the time and effort you all took, in helping me, to achieved my goal. And to those who corrected the many mistakes we came across.

Without the backing of my very understanding wife Linda, and all those endless cups of cappuccino, she supplied me with, for all the upset my family has been through over the many years because of this research and from all those questions I kept asking and for the answers I received, also the strain my business has been under and to Jerry for keeping it afloat, the many times I was away; I could never of achieved so much, if it wasn't for the people who helped me, I would like to say, here and now, without your help none of this would be possible, from the bottom of my heart I personally would like to say a big "Thank You" to you all.

I hope and pray that now
they can all
Rest in Peace

Chapter 8

Probate, Relief Fund Reports, Census & Pictorial References

(From the Western Morning News, 19th April 1912)

The Fears of Relatives

- Three inhabitants of Bodmin had relatives on board the R.M.S. Titanic. Mrs George Pidwell of Robartes Road, Southampton had a sister (Mrs Lobb), who was going out to America with her husband, also Father's Smith and Prior McElroy, of St. Mary's Roman Catholic Priory, Bodmin, had brothers aboard, the latter's brother being the chief purser of the liner.

(From the West Briton and Cornwall Advertiser, 25th April 1912)

Bodmin Priests Bereaved

- At Mass at St Piran's Roman Catholic Church in Truro, on Sunday morning, prayers were offered for those who went down with the R.M.S. Titanic, and a special mention was made of Mr Hugh McElroy, the chief purser, brother of the present Prior of Bodmin and Mr Reginald Smith one of the "R.M.S. Titanic's" engineer, brother of Farther Smith, both of whom were drowned.

Note: Father Aloysuis Smith who travelled with Richard to Southampton on hearing of the disaster and who also had a brother aboard R.M.S. Titanic, Reginald George Smith who was a Saloon Steward, not an engineer, as was stated in the West Briton and Cornwall Advertiser.

(From the Coventry Standard, 26th – 27th April 1912)

Irish Priests Lost

- Amongst various stories of church services after the disaster, Roman Catholic priest of St Mary's Church in Coventry; on Sunday morning Reverend R. F. Rea said in church that amongst those lost were two Irish priests and a number of good Catholics belonging to the crew including Chief Purser Hugh McElroy (sic), whose two sisters were educated at St

- Joseph's Convent, Gosford Green in Coventry, where also their mother remained in residence at that time.

(From the 1871 Census, Liverpool)

- 1871 Census shows both Hugh's Mother and Father shared their home with Jessie's sister Charlotta Lucy Fox who was aged 29, she had moved from 14, Georges Square, St Cuthbert, Edinburgh, Midlothian after a request from Jessie, to come and stay, while they set up home, there was also a General Domestic, Ann Jane Corlett who was from Castletown, on the Isle of Man she was aged 28

- Hugh Richard McElroy was born at 3, Percy Street, Liverpool on 28th October 1874. He was the son of Richard R. McElroy and Jessie (formerly Fox)

(From the 1881 Census, Liverpool)

- 1881 Census (taken 3rd April 1881), Hugh was living at 6, Eversley Street, Toxteth, Liverpool with his Father, Richard (36) born in Liverpool, who was described as a ships carpenter and his mother Jessie (33) born in Edinburgh. Also at home was Hugh's younger brother Richard McElroy aged 3, he was born in Liverpool, (It was Richard who was to become a Catholic Priest and who held the position of Prior at St Mary's Church in Bodmin, Cornwall at the time of the tragedy), also Rose Kingsley (34) Nurse/ Domestic Servant.

- Charlotte aged 7 and Josephine aged 5, were not shown on the 1881 Census, as they were attending St Joseph's Convent, Gosford Green in Coventry as boarders receiving a convent education. And would have been included on the 1881 Census for St Joseph's Convent.

(From the Census Returns for Cotton College 1881)

- Aloysuis (Alfred) SMITH. Boarder. U. Male 13 years. Birmingham, Warwick, England. Student

(From the 1891 Census, Liverpool)

- 1891 Census it shows Bridget (Ireland) aged 70, at 37a, Shaw Street, Everton, (living on her own means). She had a 17 year old boarder, John Wilson, who worked as a clerk and was from Ireland (she possibly took in a boarder to help offset the bills) there were also two General Domestic, Mary Ellison who was from Liverpool, aged 50 and Mary MacCabe also from Liverpool, aged 27 years. Bridget died in Liverpool, on the 8th November 1897, aged 77 years. (It has been spoken of many times, "Hugh's Irish ancestry"; His Grandmother Bridget was the only Irish descendent in his family.)

- 1891 Census, Hugh's sister, Charlotte, who was then 19 years of age, the year before, had taken a job, as a Governess, to seven children (1 boy and 6 girls, their age ranging from 9 years to 12 months old) of Mr & Mrs William Orlagh (General Practitioner), his wife Bertha was from Liverpool, there was also four domestic servants, at 49, Grange Wood Lodge, Ashby-de-la-Zouch, Bosworth, Leicester.

(From the 1901 Census, Liverpool)

- Just after Hugh's father died in 1888 the family moved across the River Mersey, to 6, Wilton Street, Liscard, Wirral.

- 1901 Census it shows only Jessie (mother), Charlotte, Hugh and Richard also a domestic Rose Fox from Leitrim, Ireland. Josephine (Hugh's sister) is not shown at 6, Wilton Street, because she died, aged 26 on 4th October 1899, before the Census was taken.

Probate Report states:

- McElroy, Hugh Walter of Polygon House, Southampton. Ship's Purser. Administration: London 31st July 1912 to Mrs Barbara McElroy widow, effects £4330. 13. 3d.

(From the Mansion House R.M.S. Titanic Relief Fund Booklet, March 1913).

- Case Number 512. McElroy, Jessie, (mother). Barbara (Nee Ennis), (widow) and Charlotte, (sister), all class "A" dependants.

(From the Minute Book of the Southampton Committee of the R.M.S. Titanic Relief Fund, November 1914)

- Case Number 512. McElroy. The dependants in this case were the widow and the mother. The widow has since remarried and therefore off the Fund. The occupation of the deceased was Purser, and he allowed his mother £240 per annum, his wife had a separate estate. The widow recognized that the scheme did not meet the equity of the case as between herself and mother, and she therefore voluntarily paid out of her widow's allowance 7/6d per week in augmentation of 7/6d per week paid from the Fund. Since the remarriage of the widow however, this special arrangement has ceased, leaving the mother who is a widow, solely dependent upon the Fund allowance. In view of these facts the Committee considers the case of Mrs. McElroy, (mother) as one of comparative hardship and recommend payment of supplementary grant at the rate of 7/6d per week. The dependent is now 66 years of age.

- 1914. Authorized from January 1915, Dated 3rd December 1914.

(The R.M.S. Titanic Relief Fund, Minute Book number 2, Southampton Area)

- From Case number 512. That the widowed mothers allowance be increased to 10/—per week for life.

(From the Atlantic Daily Bulletin 4/1999)

- Hugh Walter McElroy was born on 28th October 1874 at 3, Percy Street, Liverpool, the son of Richard McElroy, and his wife Jessie (nee Fox). On Hugh's certificate his father's occupation is shown as Shipbuilder, (he was a ships carpenter) and he was known as "Captain McElroy", although this may have been an honorary title.

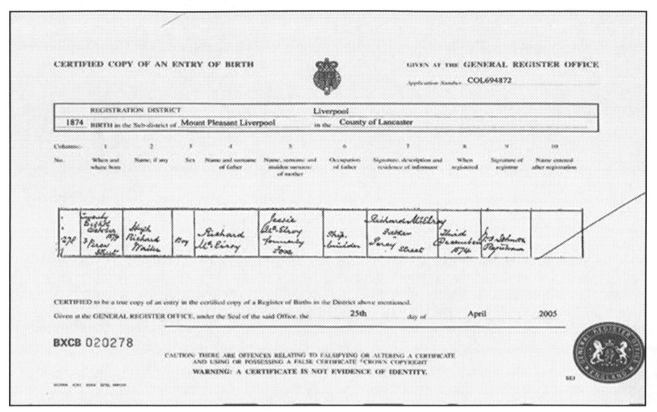

Hugh's birth Certificate

Street name plate, Percy Street

3, Percy Street, Liverpool

Eversley Street, Liverpool, Street name plate

6, Eversley Street as it is today

Street name plate Wilton Street, Liscard.

6, Wilton Street, Liscard, Wirral.

St Mary's Abbey and Church in Bodmin, Cornwall

Interior of the Church of St Mary's, Bodmin,

The frontage of St Mary's Priory, Bodmin,

Cotton Hall Ecclesiastical College, near Oakamoor, Staffordshire England

Cotton College Theatre & Hall in St Thomas' (1913) where Hugh performed on stage, in one of the many kind of humorous plays that they seemed to put on.

Cotton, St Thomas' Theatre & Hall, before the college was locked up and left in a rundown state, today the College has been vandalized and is awaiting a demolition order.

Dormitory corridor, Hugh's Dorm was first on the left; these photos were taken before the College was vandalized.

This was Hugh's dormitory, according to the pupil intake Hugh's bed would have been on the right, in the corner

Hugh's First Form Classroom at St Thomas's

Hugh's Second Form Classroom at St Thomas's

The Main Dinning Room, at St Thomas's Cotton College for all Pupils, Masters, Clergy and Nuns

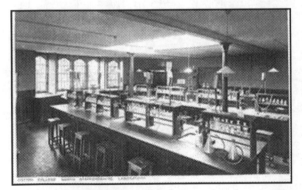

The Laboratory for the Second year pupils

The Library for both First and Second year pupils

Sanctuary inside
St Winifred's
Church

Cotton Hall as it was in 1914

The Cloister at
Cotton College

On the 12th April 1912, Hugh sent a Marconigram to his friend Fishwick; the Purser of the SS Empress of Britain, seen here entering the dry dock in Southampton in 1935, in the background is the R.M.S. Olympic awaiting her fate to be scraped.

Jessie (Mother)   Richard (Brother)   Charlotte (Sister—Nan)

Hugh (age 12 – at home)   Frankie's Mum and Dad

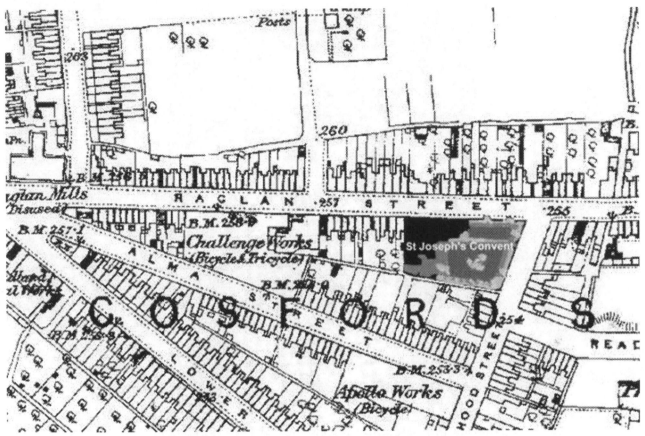

St. Joseph's Convent, at Gosford Green. Coventry

Grandpops and Nan (Charlotte)
on their Wedding day

Author (Frankie) and his sister
taken in Liverpool, 1955

Hugh in Purser's uniform showing the Transport Medal
with the South African ribbon for the clasp, in 1909

*The Novitiate in 1890 (l. to r.) Front: Egerton Beck. Philip Corr.
Centre: Tipping. Thomas Belton, CRL. Novice Master. Cuthbert
McAdam. Back: Elliot. Hugh McElroy. Rota. (Hugh McElroy
became chief purser on the Titanic and went down with her.)*

THE NEW YORK TIMES, MONDAY, MAY 4, 1903.

THE CEDRIC'S PARROT MASCOT

"Baden-Powell" Won Purser McElroy's Heart by Sighting a "Landlubber off the Starboard"

Not since the days of Funston the famous Mexican parrot of Castle William on Governors Island, has there been seen in these parts a bird so wonderfully intelligent as is Baden-Powell, the big white or the Australian parrot whose home is on the White Star liner Cedric. The other day when the Cedric sailed out of New York bound for Liverpool, there stood at the rail waving farewell to friends ashore a big well-built Scotchman named McElroy and on his shoulder there perched a great white parrot, McElroy is Cedric's purser and Baden-Powell is his ward.

Purser McElroy was for several years past acting as purser on the White Star liner Britannic, one of the vessels of that lines fleet requisitioned into service by the British Government as a transport for the South African service. It was just after the Britannic became a military transport that McElroy ran across Baden-Powell. The bird arrived in Cape Town one day on a tramp steamer. McElroy was strolling along the docks when suddenly the air was rent with the cry, "Landlubber off the starboard!" McElroy looked around and he caught the eye of the parrot, and then the feathered wonder piped, "He's rubbered."

Right then and there McElroy made up his mind to secure the bird and going on board he enquired for the owner. He was escorted to the cabin of one of the junior officers, who pleaded guilty to owning the bird. "I want him, and just simply have got to have him," was the way Britannica's purser opened negotiations." Sorry but you can't have him," was the laconic refusal of the owner. Then McElroy worked on the officer's patriotism by telling him what a joy the bird would be to the thousands of soldiers who were destined to journey to and from England on the Britannic.

"All right" answered the owner of the bird, "I will let you have him on one condition. His name now is Petroleum Pete, since Petroleum is what we carry principally, and I don't like that name, you must call him Baden-Powell," the bargain was concluded. Petroleum Pete was reregistered according to contract, and an hour later was safely caged away in McElroy's cabin aboard the Britannic.

When the Cedric arrived in New York on her last trip Baden-Powell was not on deck when the big liner was berthed neither was his guardian. When found he was perched on McElroy's shoulder, the officer being busy in his office getting his papers ready to be turned over to the proper officials. An acquaintance of McElroy knocked at the door." Keep out No lobsters wanted", was what the knocker on the outside heard from within, "Shut up, Baden, Come in it's alright" answered McElroy, and the friend opened the door. McElroy greeted his friend warmly while Baden-Powell with a look of disdain on his peaked countenance eyed him critically.

"Bum looker, don't eat much ice," piped the parrot. McElroy told the bird to shut up and where upon Baden-Powell gave a loud "All right, all right" and leaving his place on McElroy shoulder, took up his position on the windowsill overlooking the grand stairway.

"Look out Mac; the old man's coming!" said Baden-Powell. I told you to shut up retorted the purser, "All right answered Baden-Powell and obeyed orders.

WEDDING GIFT ON SCALES

Package Containing Pearl Necklace Full Weight

Broken Seal on Covering of Cuba's President to Miss Alice Aroused Suspicion of Customs Inspector

Cuba's wedding present to Miss Alice Roosevelt a splendid pearl necklace costing about $25,000 and manufactured by a firm of Parisian jewellers, arrived today aboard the White Star liner Majestic, in charge of the, purser McElroy, who had received it from a representative of the American Express Company at Liverpool for transportation to the city. The package containing the necklace was bound with cord and sealed with six wax seals. A seal on one corner was slightly cracked, and the cord was a bit loose when the package was handed over to Customs Inspector Moore, just just after the liner docked, He viewed it with unusual circumspection, and discovering the slight crack naturally was anxious to have so precious a thing as a package containing a gift to the daughter of the President in proper shape when it left his hands, and insisted that it should be weighed.

According to the bill of lading the weight of the package when it was shipped was six pounds one and one-half ounces. It was put on a pair of scales on the pier for weighing bulky material, and apparantly was one and a half pounds less than the bill of lading called for, Moore believed that the package had been tampered with. Then the package was weighed at the office of the express company and showed not a variation of a fraction of an ounce from the weight named on the bill of lading.

The package was dispatched to Washington in care of a special messenger who will turn it over to the Cuban Minister.

Foreign Manage Berry, of the express company, said there was no doubt that the necklace was all right, and that there been no attempt to tamper with the package.

The bill of lading read: 'To His Excellency the Minister of Cuba, No. 1000 Sixteen street, Washington, D.C.

"One case containing a box with six red pearls of the Cuban consul in Paris: one pearl necklace, value 128,175 francs, no duty being imposed, Recieved from the Minister of Cuba in Paris, bound to Georgetown.D.C; steamship Majestic; insurance, $81.96; weighing six pounds one and one-half ounces."

© The Washington Post : Friday February 16th 1906

The New York Times.
Thursday, October 25 1906

RUNAWAYS WED IN MID OCEAN

A Romantic Marriage of Swedish Immigrants on the Majestic

Passengers on the White Star Liner Majestic which arrived yesterday afternoon witnessed in mid-Atlantic the wedding of two Swedish immigrants. The happy couple were Wilfred Larsen and Elizabeth Wickstrand both natives of Bronten, Sweden

The Rev. R. C. Williams performed the ceremony last Monday morning in the Pursers Office. The entry in the official log book was signed, as witnessed by Senator W. A. Clark of Montana, J. E. Hargreaves, Justice of the Peace of Westmoreland, England, and Captain Bertrand P. Hayes of the Majestic. After the Wedding the newly wedded pair had a reception in the saloon and a toast to their health and future prosperity was proposed by Senator Clark and drunk by the passengers. A wedding cake had been prepared for the occasion by the ship's chief baker C. Russell and a purse was subscribed by the salon passengers and given to the bridegroom. The compatriots of the couple in the steerage kept the fun up till early on Tuesday morning.

What interested everybody aboard was the romance of the match. Wickstrand were sweethearts from childhood in Bronten. Their parents opposed the match so they at last made up their minds to run away to America and get married. Some of their friends on board the Majestic suggested that there might be an order to stop them on arrival at Ellis Island so they decided to be married at sea and land as man and wife. Capt Hayes who had had twenty four years experience in the White Star service said this was the first time he had witnessed a marriage on the Atlantic. In the sailing ship days to Australia and New Zealand it was a common occurrence but not on the short trip from Liverpool to New York.

'Runaways wed in mid ocean'
A Romantic Marriage of Swedish Immigrants on the Majestic.
[New York Times (DN) /-Current file].
New York, N.Y.: Oct 25, 1906. pg. 9. 1 pgs.
Document types: marriage.
ISSN/ISBN: 03624331.
Text Word Count: 30

The incident involving Hugh on 25th October 1906, aboard the SS. Majestic, in which a young couple from Bronten in Sweden ran away to America to start a new life.

The research for this started in a book named "Hull Down" written by Captain Bertrand P. Hayes, who was the Captain of the Majestic.

A photograph was taken afterwards on the saloon deck by the Majestic's doctor, with Captain Hayes camera and when the captain later looked for the film, found it had been taken from the camera by the doctor and sold to a New York newspaper, the photograph together with a long account of the ceremony, appeared in the press the next morning after they arrived in America.

MONTANA MAN IS SPONSOR AT A HAPPY OCEAN WEDDING

The original story with regards to a Sweedish couple marrying aboard the RMS Majestic, first appeared in The New York Times on Thursday 27th October 1906 under the heading "Runaways Wed in Mid-Ocean".

The story plus photo then appeared in The Fort Wayne Evening Sentinel on Saturday, October 27th 1906.

The story later reapeared in The Anoconda Standard on Friday morning, November 9th 1906 (the two latter stories both have the same picture and same story). It was Dr Francis who Capt Haynes said stole the picture (a book wrote by Capt Haynes entitled "Hull Down" mostly about life aboard RMS Majestic).

Photo – left to right: Capt Haynes, Senator Clark, Mrs W Larson (Wickstrand), Mr Hardgreaves, Mr Wilfred Larson and Dr Francis

New York Nov 8 – Not in 25 years according to the Officers of the Majestic of the White Star Line, had a romance culminated in a marriage onboard a Trans Atlantic Liner while on the high seas until last Monday when onboard that ship Wilfred Larson a young Swede and Miss Elizabeth Wickstrand of Minneapolis were married.

Senator W. A. Clark was the witness for the Bride, while the witnesses for the bridegroom were J. E. Hardgreaves an English Magistrate and Dr Arthur Francis the Ships Surgeon, Mrs Larson told a reporter that before she came to this country more than three years ago she had become engaged to Larson, they having been playmates from children. She went back last June to visit her relatives in Sweden and while there Larson asked her to be his wife and not return to the United States, She consented but found she was considered an alien, having lived in this country for three years.

The marriage laws made difficulties and they decided to come to the United States and marry and settle here were Miss Wickstrand told her story to the ships surgeon in the latter's round he suggested they could be married onboard the vessel under the English Law and volunteered to make all the arrangements.

Capt B. F. Hayes commander of the vessel took an active interest in the matter and H. McElroy, the Purser offered the use of his office for the ceremony, in the second cabin was an American clergyman Rev R. C. Williams who readily consented to officiate, the marriage took place in the presence of Capt Hayes, Senator Clark, Mr Hargreves, the Purser and Dr Francis, after the ceremony Mr Hargreves ordered champagne in which the brides health was drunk and then went to the organ in the saloon and played Mendelssohn's wedding march.

Mr McElroy ordered the ships bakers to provide a big wedding cake, and dinner in the steerage that evening was a gala occasion, all the cabin passengers took great interest in the event and subscribed $25 to buy a wedding present for the bride.

© The Anoconda Standard, Anoconda, Montana Friday Morning, November 9th 1906

FEATHERED "JACK BINNS" SENDS WIRE-LESS MESSAGE

Mr Joseph Finley tells of wonderful parrot he found in Hartz mountains – Began by imitating finger taps on table – Then learns to tap the operator's key and send messages out from the SS. Adriatic

New York July 29th - "Mr Joseph Finley, at his home. No 494, Hulsey Street, Brooklyn, today told the story of his capture of the wonderful parrot that will arrive here sometime this week and which is now sending wireless messages with unerring aim all over the Atlantic. Mr Finley arrived on the White Star line steamship "Cedric" with two friends.

"I caught my parrot in the Hartz mountains," said Mr Finley. "He had escaped from some zoological garden in Germany. Undoubtedly, but as I could not discover the owner I kept the bird and found, after a few days, that he would imitate the taps I made on the table with my fingers, a habit I have. Later, in London, I met Mr McElroy, who is the Purser of the "Adriatic". I gave him the parrot and telling him the trick of the parrot of imitating the tapping of my fingers, it was found that he would tap the wireless key on the Adriatic just as regularly ands precisely as he did the table tap".

"As a result of some experiments, the parrot was found quite competent to send wireless messages without the regular operator touching the key, the bird simply following each tap of the operator's finger on the table with a tap on the key. He was quite precise in his imitation of the dots and dashes, and I was highly gratified in getting a wireless message on the "Cedric" which was sent "via McElroy's parrot, as the message stated."

According to Mr Finley the parrot he caught will become a second "Jack Binns" if he keeps on at the rate that he is now going. The taps on the table of the Adriatic's wireless operator's finger were instantly copied by the "wireless parrot" and repeated on the key controlling the sending of the wireless dispatches by the bird striking the key with its foot.

Advance news of the "Adriatic" may be expected today or tomorrow,, providing, of course, that Purser McElroy's parrot is in his usual good form.

The Fort Wayne Sentinel, USA
28th July 1910.

It was reported in the Fort Wayne Sentinel, USA on the 28th July 1910 that Purser Hugh McElroy had taken to Parrot Minding, the following article along with a picture of Hugh holding the parrot, it also accompanied a picture of the parrot's owner Mr Joseph Finley.

Nearly two years later, Wednesday 10th April 1912, on the RMS Titanic's maiden voyage Hugh had then taken to canary minding, the canary sailed on the Titanic and survived, it was owned by a Mr. Meanwell who lived in France and wanted to get his prize winning precious canary to Cherbourg from England. He asked the Chief Purser to carry it on the Titanic, Hugh kept the bird in his office, (the canary disembarked when the Titanic arrived in Cherbourg,

THREE COUPLES WED ON THE MAJESTIC

Immigration Law Unearths a Series of Romances When the Liner Arrives

GIRLS CAME HERE TO MARRY

Not Allowed to Land, So a Parson Tied the Knot on the Ship and the Officers Gave Them a Breakfast

The White Star liner Majestic, which arrived from Southampton late on Wednesday, was the scene of a triple wedding yesterday. A curious feature of the ceremony was that the three brides never met until they boarded the Majestic and the three bridegrooms had never heard of each other until they met in the saloon of the liner on Wednesday.

Among the second cabin passengers were three young English girls, each of whom told the immigration officials that they had come here to marry. They were Miss Alice L. Osborne of Norwich, who was betrothed to Walter R. Smith, formerly of London, but now the New York representative of an English machinery firm; Miss Mildred Hand of Bournemouth, England, who was to wed Ernest Dover, who used to live in Fordham Bridge, England,

but is now a clerk for the Interborough Railroad, and Miss Rose Jane Webb of Portsmouth, England, who as the wife of Eno Deason will live in Cleveland, Ohio.

It had been the intention of Mr. Smith and Miss Osborne to marry at the home the former has established at 502 West 172d Street, but when he learned that the Government exercised a care over young women landing here he consented to be married in the saloon of the Majestic. The situation was explained to the other two men and they agreed to be married on board. So the ship's officers and the stewards, being interested in the triple event, set out to prepare a celebration.

It was necessary before the ceremony to make a trip to the License Bureau at the City Hall, and so the happy couples were taken there under the chaperonage of Mrs. Walters, the Ellis Island matron.

The three were married by the Rev. Jacob Price of the Washington Heights Methodist Episcopal Church.

Purser Edwards gave the brides in marriage, and after the ceremony the party sat down to a wedding breakfast which had been spread in the saloon. After it was over the three couples made a tour of the city in a sight-seeing automobile. They also agreed that they would form themselves into a Majestic club with the object of holding a reunion once a year.

To an inquirer who sought their stories Miss Osborne said that she first met Mr. Smith at Yarmouth, England, and fell in love with him because of his rowing. Miss Webb said that she met Mr. Deason while visiting her sister and Miss Hand said that she met Mr. Dower so long ago that really she had forgotten [sic] just how it all happened.

The New York Times,
9 October 1908

PEABODY COUSINS WED.

Miss Katharine P. and W. Rodman Are Married by Bridegroom's Father.

With regards to getting married aboard the "RMS Majestic", seems to of started something amongst the young immigrants, before being passed through Ellis Island, because two years later, an article appeared in the New York Times on the 9th October 1908

DEATH PURSUED PURSUER

Fate Tracked Man Finally Assigned to Titanic.

New York April 19 - Geoffrey P. Rogers purser of the White Star liner Laurentic had been appointed as joint purser with McElroy, of the ill-fated Titanic, but at the last moment this was canceled. Mr Barker late of the Majestic, was ordered to the Titanic.

A coincidence is that Barker relieved Rogers when he left the Republic. Barker's life was spared when the disaster overcame the Republic, but only to lose it while vemployed on the Titanic

The Evening Independent - Massillon, Ohio
Friday April 19th 1912

TITANIC BRAVE BRAVE

Said good-bye with a smile although he knew the end was near (From the New York Sun)
G.B.McElroy, the purser of the Titanic, was very popular among his brother officers, a purser of other White Star liners was telling yesterday of what he had heard had been the last of Mac, as the other was familiarly known.
"I got it from lightoller" he said " he met the big fellow on deck, Mac was smiling "Good-bye", he said to the second officer, shaking hands. "I wish you luck" Then looking about he said still smiling "It looks as if we were going to have sand for supper".

Colorado Springs Gazette, - Colorado Springs, Colorado
Wednesday May 15th 1912

JOKED IN THE FACE OF DEATH

Last Words of Titanic's Purser, McElroy Were Lighthearted and Cheerful

Charles Brown, the English comedian lost a number of friends in the Titanic tragedy. He knew most of the officers on the ill-fated ship, and the purser, McElroy had been his comrade for years. A recent letter from England brought to the actor the last words of McElroy - an account of life which is notable for his calm British courage, the fourth officer, Mariais,who went down with the ship and was plucked up by a boat is the man who testifies to McElroy's behavior. A small group of the Titanics staff was waiting for the final plunge. The water was lapping the deck at their very feet and the end was meraly a question of a very few minutes. McElroy turned to his companions with a smile and shook hands with them saying "Well good-bye fellows; it looks like sand for breakfast tomorrow." That was typical of McElroy says Brown, He was one of the merriest bravest men who ever lived. It was like him to have a little joke in the face of death.

The Evening Telegram - Elyria, Ohio
Thursday July 11th 1912

Hugh with Barbara and little John Patrick Ennis son of Barbara's brother John) this photo was taken in Waterford, County Wexford, while they were still on honeymoon in October 1910.

The inner gateway into "Springwood"

"Springwood" the Ennis family home

The Main gateway into to the Springwood Estate

St Peters RC Church in Ballymitty, County Wexford, were Hugh and Barbara were married on Saturday 9th July 1910

The beautiful interior of St Peters church, the chalice that is still used for the Mass, was presented to St Peters church by the Ennis family in 1910

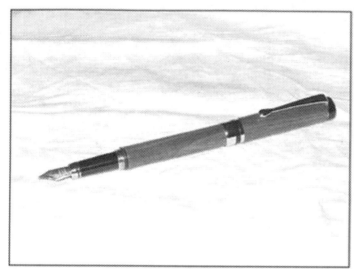

Body No 157 was tentatively identified by Research Group 1991. Description: male; estimated age 32; dark hair; Clothing: ship's uniform; white jacket; ship's keys,10 pence; 50 cents; they also found his beloved fountain pen.

Hugh is als mentioned in the "Boer War Transport Medal Roll" book, while later serving aboard the "Britannic" under the command of Captain E. J. Smith, he came to be awarded along with Captain Smith the "Transport Medal" with the South Africa clasp,; this was presented on 1st Dec 1903, by the Director of Transport. This medal was awarded to Pursers 'whose position and services specially deserved'

The Polygon in Southampton was replaced by these block of luxury flats, the builders inserted in the corner suround wall two foundations stones that came from the original building, the stone on the left was the first "Polygon" Laid 9th August 1768, right Polygon Hotel laid 22nd September 1937

Captain Smith's old house in Winn Road was called "Lyndale" which was demolished to make way for a block of flats [Cheltenham Court], it was built were his house once stood, a picture of Titanic is just inside the doorway and an inscription tells you about Captain Smith's old house. The same fate was bestowed on the "Polygon House" which in 1938 was renamed "The Polygon Hotel" and was situated at the corner of Devonshire Road and The Polygon, (and again another new block of flats was put up). They placed two stones in the wall surrounding the Flats, one from the original Polygon House, when the first laid on 9th August 1768, the second stone is from the Polygon Hotel and this was laid on 22nd September 1937, also the White Star Line's main building in Liverpool was actually addressed, White Star Line, "Albion House", 30, James Street, Liverpool, Lancashire.

© DK

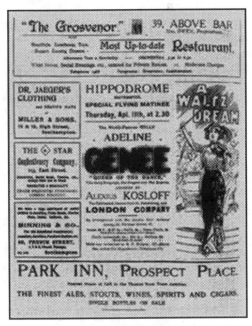

©Park Lane Posters

On E" Deck was the Assistant Purser's Office, organized by the 40 year old Assistant Purser Reginald L. Baker,

Before Titanic sailed on the Wednesday 10th April 1912, Hugh and his wife Barbara sent a bouquet of flowers to Mdlle Adeline Genee

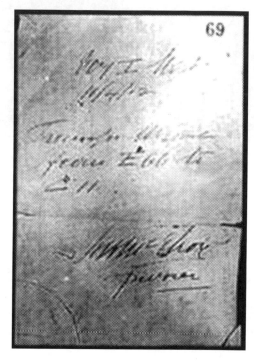

The page from the log of the Majestic, which was Used for the marriage of Wilfred Larsen and Elizabeth Wickstrand and appeared in the New York Times on Thursday, 25th October 1906

Hugh handed the Steward his note of authorization for the changeover and asked him to attend to the matter, Faulkner read the note, pocketed it and carried out the instruction, another happy passenger.

CERTIFICATE OF MARRIAGE

Parish of _Bannow_   Diocese of _Ferns_

EXTRACT FROM THE MARRIAGE REGISTER

Hugh McElroy and

Barbara Ennis

were married in the Church of _Carrig on Bannow,_

Co. Wexford according to the Rite of the Catholic Church,

on the _9th_ day of _July_ 19_10_

The Witnesses were _J. Keogh_

and _Edith Ennis_

Rev. _Jim Kehoe_   Parish Priest Curate

L.S.

Date _9-2-07._

Hugh and Barbara's Marriage Certificate

The designated tables in Titanic's First Class Restaurant

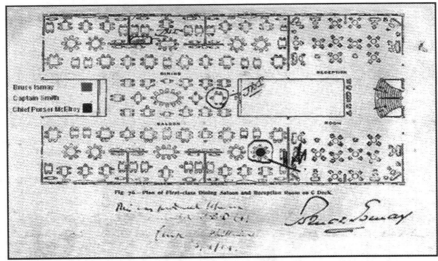

© Encyclopedia Titanica

The Titanic's First Class Restaurant had tables that were designated, Bruce Ismay had a two-seater table (Red) but preferred to dine alone, Captain Smith had a six/eight seated table (Green) and Chief Purser Hugh McElroy always had an eight-seated table (Blue).

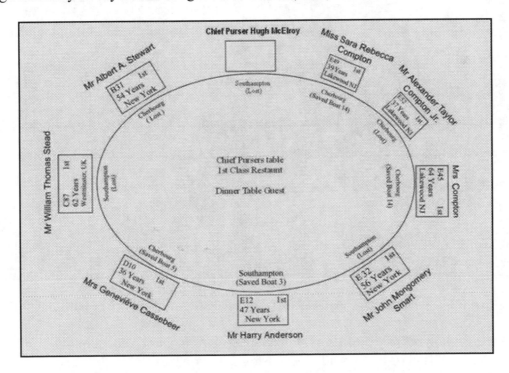

The placement of the dinner companions for Hugh's last dinner aboard the R.M.S. Titanic on Sunday April 14th 1912, from his left was Miss Sara Rebecca Compton, Mr Alexander Taylor Compton Jr and Mrs Compton from Lakewood New Jersey, USA, who was sitting next to Mr John Montgomery Smart of New York he was sitting next to another New Yorker Mr Harry Anderson, then came Mrs Geneviève Cassebeer who was also a New Yorker and to her left was Mr William Thomas Stead from Westminster, London and the last dinner companions was Mr Albert A. Stewart who had homes in both Paris and New York.

Photographs taken onboard the R.M.S. Titanic

© Cork Examiner / Mr Thomas Baker   (Hugh looks Official and stiff upper lip)

© Father Francis Browne Collection   (Hugh looks Unofficial and relaxed)

These are the last pictures taken of Hugh with Captain Smith, Captured, aboard Titanic when she was anchor just outside Queenstown harbour off the Irish coast.

Hugh's signature

87

(© Public Archives of Nova Scotia)
Titanic's lifeboats making way, to Carpathia

(© Public Archives of Nova Scotia)
The Titanic last lifeboat, being rescued

(© Public Archives of Nova Scotia)
The crew of the McKay Bennet

(© Public Archives of Nova Scotia)
Crew of the McKay Bennet, retrieving a body from the RMS Titanic

This photograph was taken onboard the "London Brighton & South Coast Railroad" cross-channel steamer "S.S. Paris" (Newport-Dieppe route) about 1910

John Hemmert (Texas) © Orlando Titanic Museum

(Left to Right) Jessie (Mother), Charlotte (Sister), Alice (Barbara's niece), Barbara (Wife), Hugh, Chief Engineer Bell, Jonathan Lipton (Cousin to Thomas Lipton the Tea Magnet), Harold Turner & Helen Vanderbilt (She's the one wearing a WSL Officers cap, probably from the fellow who took the picture.

Notes: I found this photo in a local junk shop. I'd just finished flipping through "An Illustrated History of Titanic" and I recognized Hugh in the photo immediately. So, I bought the photo and researched it for 6 months before turning it over to the Orlando Titanic Museum The place I got the photo from, had a lot of stuff bought from the estate of Neil Vanderbilt (The "fifth"), the Godson of J.P. Morgan. (*John Hemmer*)

Cross-Channel steamer "S.S. Paris" (Newport-Dieppe route)

Hugh and the Officers of the R.M.S. Olympic

(Standing L to R) 1st Officer William Murdoch, Purser Hugh McElroy,
Purser Claude Lancaster, 2nd Officer Robert Hume
(Seated L to R) Captain Edward. J. Smith and Dr William F. N. O'Loughlin

"Captain Smith and the Officers of the R.M.S. Olympic"

(Back row standing) Purser Hugh Walter McElroy, 3rd Officer Henry Osborne Cater, 2nd Officer
Robert Hume, 4th Officer David William Alexander and 6th Officer Harold Holehouse.
(Front row seated) 5th Officer Alphonse Martin Tulloch, Chief Officer Joseph Evans, Captain
Edward John Smith, and 1st Officer William McMaster Murdoch.

Notes from Inger Sheil,
The above picture has been misidentified as the Titanic's Officers for many years, and it was reproduced in several books, and on numerous websites. In addition, individual heads have been taken out and reproduced, captioned as various Titanic Officers, I think the reason it has been misidentified as the Titanic's Officers is, the fact that it includes Officer William Murdoch and Captain E.J. Smith, as well as Purser Hugh McElroy. Somebody "WANTED" it to be the Titanic's Officers, and after positively identifying the aforementioned three men, simply counted stripes on sleeves and wouldn't the one in the middle with the 'stache be Pitman . . . and so on.

Inger Sheil wrote an article for the "Atlantic Daily Bulletin" (the British Titanic Society's research journal) identifying the chaps correctly. There was also an article in the "Titanic Commutator" Vol. 24, No. 151, 2000, about the misidentification of these Officers.

(Standing L to R) 6th Officer Harold Holehouse, Dr William F. N. O'Loughlin, Assistant Surgeon Dr A White, 5th Officer Alphonse Martin Tulloch, 2nd Officer Robert Hume, 4th Officer David William Alexander, Chief Officer Henry Tingle Wilde *(partly obscured)*, Captain Edward J. Smith, Purser Claude Lancaster, Chief Engineer Robert Fleming, 3rd Officer Henry Osborne Cater, 1st Officer William Mc Master Murdoch, Purser Hugh Walter Richard McElroy.

1st Officer William Murdoch, Chief Officer Henry Wilde,
5th Officer Harold Lowe and Captain E. J. Smit

Census Forms

1871 English Census, (taken 2nd April 1871) showing Richard and Jessie, who were residing at 9, Cheshire Crescent, along with Charlotta L. Fox (Jessie's sister) and Ann Jane Corlett (Servant)

1881 English Census, (taken 3rd April 1881) showing Barbara's family, who resided at 5, Derwent Road, Liverpool. (Father & Mother) John and Elizabeth; Barbara M; (sister) Edith M; (Brother) John; (Aunt) Barbara & (cousin) Dora Cousins also residing at this address are sister's Martha and Margaret Cardiff (servants)

1881 English Census, (taken 3rd April 1881) showing Richard and Jessie, who were residing at 6, Eversley Street, along with Hugh and Richard (Hugh's younger brother) also Rose Kingsley (Nurse/ Domestic Servant) Charlotte & Josephine, were in convent residence at St Joseph's Convent, Gosford Green in Coventry.

1891 English Census, (taken 5th April 1891) showing Bridget (70), who was residing at 37a, Shaw Street, Everton, Liverpool, along with John Wilson (17) who was a boarder, Mary Elison (50) and Mary MacCabe (27)

1901 English Census (taken 31st March 1901) for 6, Wilton Street, it shows only Jessie (mother), Charlotte, Hugh and Richard also a General Domestic, Rose Fox from Leitrim in Ireland, Josephine died on the 4th October 1899.

RG 12 / 2509

RG 12 / 2509

In the 1891 Census, (taken 5th April 1891) Hugh's sister, Charlotte, who was then 19 years of age, had taken a job, as a Governess, working for a General Practitioner, he had just moved from Manchester, to 49, Grange Wood Lodge, Ashby-de-la-Zouch, Bosworth, Leicester, to take up a position as GP in a larger practice that was well established.

1891 English Census, (taken 5th April 1891) show's Richard (Hugh's younger brother) (No 9) at Cotton Hall College, aged 14 years

Crew of the Californian summoned to give evidence at the British Inquiry, among those pictured are wireless operator Cyril Evans (5th from left), Apprentice James Gibson (3rd from left) and Second Officer Herbert Stone (4th from left) also (2nd from left) is Captain Stanley Lord, waiting outside the Scottish Drill Hall where the British Inquiry was held, Captain Stanley Lord was unfairly made the scapegoat by both inquiries ruining his career. In the British Inquiry Final Report indicated that the Officers of the Californian had indeed seen the rockets of the Titanic through the rigging, but that any fault in failing to act lay with Second Officer Herbert Stone.

1911 Census of Ireland Return
Family Name: John Ennis
Address: "Springwood", Tullycanna, Wexford
Order Number ENE1317928436

Details from Form B1—House and Building Return

1. John Ennis and 16 other persons occupied a private dwelling with 15 out offices. The walls were built of stone, brick or concrete with a roof of slate, iron or tile. There were 10 occupied rooms in the house with 9 windows at the front of the building. It was recorded as a 1st class house.

Form A

Name	Position in House	Religion	Education	Age	Occupation	Marital Status	Place of Birth
John Ennis	Head	Roman Catholic	Read & Write	75	Retried Steamship manager	Widower	Wexford
Aidan Ennis	Brother	Roman Catholic	Read & Write	70	Farmer	Single	Wexford
John Ennis	Son	Roman Catholic	Read & Write	31		Married	England
Mary Ennis	Daughter-in-law	Roman Catholic	Read & Write	30		Married	England
John Ennis	Grandson	Roman Catholic	Cannot Read	3		Single	Wexford
Aidan Ennis	Grandson	Roman Catholic	Cannot Read	2		Single	Wexford
Barbara Ennis	Granddaughter	Roman Catholic	Cannot Read	1month		Single	Wexford
Barbara Canavan	Sister	Roman Catholic	Read & Write	65		Widow	Wexford
Hugh McElroy	Son-in-law	Roman Catholic	Read & Write	36	Purser	Married	England
Barbara McElroy	Daughter	Roman Catholic	Read & Write	34		Married	England
Edith Ennis	Daughter	Roman Catholic	Read & Write	33		Single	England
Ellen Kehoe	Servant	Roman Catholic	Read & Write	21	General Domestic	Single	Wexford
Mary Kehoe	Servant	Roman Catholic	Read & Write	18	General Domestic	Single	Wexford
Bridget Murphy	Servant	Roman Catholic	Read & Write	22	General Domestic	Single	Wexford
James Keane	Servant	Roman Catholic	Cannot Read	64	Stable man	Married	Wexford
Cathleen O'Brien	Nurse	Roman Catholic	Read & Write	42	Nurse	Single	Wexford
John Keogh	Family Friend	Roman Catholic	Read & Write	38		Married	Wexford

The Ennis family no longer live at "Springwood" anymore the estate was sold to Mr & Mrs John Nolan, Aidan Ennis who is a Jesuit Priest in Dublin and is the only remaining member of the Ennis family, as Louise Ennis died in November 1987 and therefore "Springwood" was sold after her death.

Nan's cottage "Layton" in Spettisbury in Dorset

Hugh in the Daily Mirror on April 17th 1912

Violet Jessop's original Grave in Hartest Churchyard, and her new grave stone, replaced in 2007

Violet Jessop's thatched cottage "Maythorn" in Wetherden, Great Ashfield, Suffolk.

1911, Ranelagh Street and Liverpool Central Station, with Renshaw Street at the top with Lewis's Store, and opposite the Adelphi Hotel

Photo: (from left to right 7th person, black coat, white neck band and black hat) standing together, Charlotte (Nana), Charlotte's (tall) friend Roseanna and Bridget (Great Grandma) on the Mersey foot passenger ferryboat in 1889

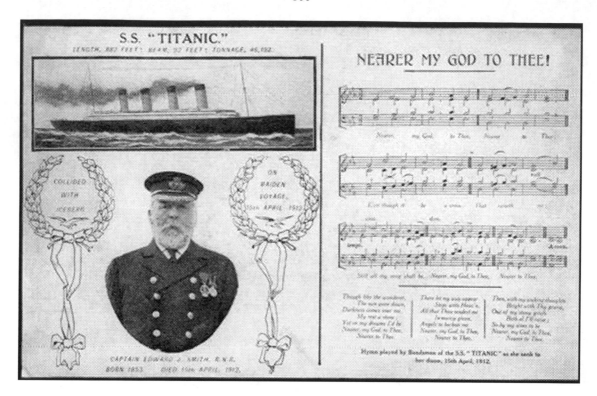

These two post cards were given to Frankie by his Nan, who was going to send them to The Mother Superior at St Joseph's Convent, Gosford Green in Coventry and also to her Sister Charlotta, who had been ill and would not of known about the sinking. But for what ever her reason, Charlotte never got to write the cards, they were put in a draw and left.

This man was the driving force behind my research, my cousin George McElroy (God bless you)

This was the last boat Frankie was aboard "Herald of free Enterprise", which Capsized 6 March 1987 and he has sworn never to step foot on any other boat, that night was one never to be forgotten, Frankie was on a day trip with his wife and family, Thank God no-one in his group was loss that night, only his daughter, after that night, he has ever ventured aboard a boat, (cruise ship around the Mediterranean).

"Raise the Titanic"

These photos were taken, of the model RMS Titanic that was used in the film "Raise the Titanic, The film was produced in 1980 at Mediterranean Film Studios, in Malta (http://mfsstudio.com)

And these photos were taken in 2008 all that is left of the rusting remains.

Titanic at the Movies

1912 Saved from the Titanic . . . . staring Dorothy Gibson (A survivor from RMS Titanic)
1912 In Nacht und Eis (In Night and Ice"), Silent Movie
1943 Titanic . . . . This was a Nazi propaganda film
1953 Titanic . . . . staring Barbara Stanwych & Robert Wagner
1956 A night to remember (television)
1958 A night to remember . . . . staring Kenneth More
1964 The Unsinable Molly Brown . . . Musical staring Debbie Reynolds
1979 S.O.S. Titanic . . . . staring David Janssen
1980 Raise the Titanic . . . . staring Richard Jordan & Alec Guinness
1995 Titanica a documentary narrated by Leonard Nimoy (Mr Spock)
1996 Titanic (television)
1997 Titanic . . . . Staring Leonardo DeCaprio & Kate Winslet
2003 Ghosts of the Abyss

Chapter 9

"The Cottonian"

St Wilfrins College—Newsletter

(Vol 2—No1) Midsummer 1912

Præsta nobis propitius ut ejus semper patrocinio adjuvemur

The Cottonian

St Wilfrid's College

Oakamoor

Vol. 2. No. 1.
Midsummer
1912.

"THE COTTONIAN" MAGAZINE.

Three Issues are published each year, at Midsummer, Christmas & Easter. The Annual Subscription is 2s. 6d. Post Free, and should be paid in advance at the commencement of each year.

SINGLE NUMBERS, 1/-

The Manager will be pleased to repurchase Copies of Vol. I., Nos. 1 and 2.

All MSS. should be addressed to the Editor, and business communications to the Manager :—

Rev. F. J. SUMNER,
St. Wilfrid's College,
Oakamoor, N. Staffs.

THE LATE HUGH McELROY,
Chief Purser SS. *Titanic.*

THE COTTONIAN.

| Vol. II. | MIDSUMMER, 1912. | No. 1. |

EDITORIAL.

THE photograph which we publish on the opposite page is a sad memorial of that appalling disaster which last April plunged two great nations into mourning. Few, indeed, were the households whose members were not called upon to suffer a personal loss or bear a vicarious grief. For ourselves we mourn the loss of one whom any college might well be proud to number amongst her sons,—a good Catholic, successful because he was a man, popular because he was a gentleman. If in the inscrutable decrees of Providence it pleased God to cut short a promising career, we can at least thank Him that he had the grace to die a noble death, and we can write, not on the unstable waters of his grave, but on the lasting tablets of our memory, those beautiful words penned in the hour of trial:

" Tears for the dead! But through that bitter rain

  Breaks like an April sun the smile of pride."

We had hoped to be able to publish an article from the pen of Mr. James J. Morgan, British Consul at Monastir, but the Albanian rising, followed by the mutiny of the garrison troops, has evidently left him little leisure for literary pursuits. We have, however, been more fortunate in the response to the appeal we made to our readers for information regarding old Cottonians for the "Old Boys' Corner," and for this we beg to thank our many correspondents.

We particularly wish to draw our readers' attention to the letter from Major Edward Hogan, President of the London Circle of the Catenian Association. As far as we can gather ours is the first school magazine to advocate the claims of this new venture, and we feel sure that our readers, old and young, will realize both the importance of this Association and the appropriateness of its finding a place in these pages. Whether as increasing the solidarity of the Catholic business world on the one hand, or, on the other, of facilitating the entrance into business of our young Catholic men, we think the work of the Association deserves the co-operation and active support of all those who have at heart the best interests of the trades and professions patronized by the middle classes.

Of the long list of prizes, both for studies and for games, which we are privileged to announce in this number and to which we tender to the donors our most grateful thanks, one only has perforce been left unawarded, owing principally to the vagaries of our English climate. We refer to the two bats offered to the batsmen who should achieve a partnership of over a hundred runs for any wicket in an out-match. Although there are still some out-matches to be played, the rain-ruined state of our wicket does not offer much chance to any of our players of making the required runs.

We beg to acknowledge with thanks the receipt of the following exchange magazines:—*Edmundian, Denstonian, St. Pancras College Chronicle, Beaumont Review, Ushaw Magazine, Lisbonian, Ratcliffian, Oscotian, Georgian, Stonyhurst Magazine, Breda, Ampleforth Journal, Albanian* and *Raven* together with the *Universe* and the *Annals of the Propagation of the Faith.*

The statement of accounts which the Hon. Manager submitted to the meeting of the St.

THE COTTONIAN.

Wilfrid's and Parkers' Society at Whitsuntide, shows that the Magazine has had a very successful first year. With a circulation which is slowly but surely increasing, we have every reason to predict a continuance of this success, if our subscribers will assist us by paying their subscriptions promptly, and, whenever possible, by patronizing our advertisers.

OLD BOYS' CORNER.

THE LATE HUGH McELROY.

HUGH McElroy, the Chief Purser of the ill-fated *Titanic*, one of the gallant men who remained at the post of duty but unhappily did not survive the dreadful wreck, will be remembered perhaps by an older generation of Cottonians.

Born in Liverpool in October, 1874, Hugh McElroy, after passing through a preparatory school, St. Mary's Lodge, St. Leonards-on-Sea, came to Cotton Hall in 1885 and remained until 1888. On one or more occasions, though but a youngster, he took part with success in the College plays, and even then gave evidence of a talent for pourtraying the humourous which in after life made him very popular as a ship's officer.

Leaving Cotton in 1888 he was sent to a private school at that time conducted by the Canons Regular in Dorsetshire, with whom he remained until 1892. In that year he commenced his business career with the Allan Line in Liverpool, where his family for two generations had been well known in shipping circles. He went to sea for the first time in 1893 as Purser of the Allan Liner *Numidian*, and continued to serve the Allan Line in the same capacity in other vessels of their fleet until the year 1899, when he joined the White Star Line. His record of service with the latter line is unique. After " trooping " throughout the Boer War, for which he received the transport medal, he was rapidly promoted as new and larger liners were added to the fleet, and it may be mentioned as evidence of the trust and confidence reposed in him, that he took the maiden voyage successively in the *Cedric*, the *Republic*, which opened the Boston-Mediterranean service, the vessel which, it may be remembered, afterwards foundered in mid-Atlantic, though all hands were happily saved through the instrumentality of wireless telegraphy (the first occasion on which it was used in this connection), the *Baltic*, the *Laurentic*, which inaugurated the White Star Canadian Service, the *Olympic*, and unfortunately, the *Titanic*.

That he was popular also with passengers is amply borne out by extracts from periodicals published after the wreck. The writer of " Motley Notes," in the *Sketch* of April 24th, makes the following reference: "When I crossed from New York to Plymouth on the *Adriatic* just before Christmas, 1910, McElroy was the Chief Purser of that vessel . . . . . I described McElroy very briefly in these notes; here is the description: ' Seven of us,' I wrote, ' sit together at meals, and I fancy we are the merriest table in the saloon. At the head sits one of the chief officers. He is so modest a fellow that I will forbear to name him; but let me hint that he is famous among all those who go down to the sea in ships as a first-class raconteur.' . . . . Big, jolly, courteous, human to the last inch, McElroy was the ideal man for the position he held."

The Liverpool *Journal of Commerce* of May 8th contained the following notice: " It has been said that so pronounced was the popularity of Mr. H. W. McElroy, the *Titanic's* Purser, that many people, who frequently crossed the Atlantic, would time their voyages so as to sail on the same ship with him. He was the Commodore Purser of the Line, and was widely known in Liverpool. A characteristic story is told of Mr. McElroy. He was last seen on the deck of the *Titanic* having under his charge bags containing the ship's papers. He was talking cheeringly and encouragingly to his three assistants. When the last lifeboat had left the ship, and Mr. McElroy had bidden 'Good-bye' to those on board, he turned to his assistants and said: 'Well, boys, the last boat has gone. I'm afraid we must eat sand for supper to-night.'"

The Western Daily Mercury published another account taken from a survivor on the arrival of the *Lapland* at Plymouth: "A stirring story concerns the closing chapter of the career of Chief Purser McElroy. From the outset Mr. McElroy was kept busily employed rousing the passengers and then encouraging them to face the ordeal that awaited them. From one to the other he went with characteristic sang-froid and coolness, his cheery manner giving heart to many. Here he stopped to fasten a lifebelt a little more securely; there it was to persuade a passenger to put on warmer clothing. Then he conducted them to the boats, and as the last one drew away from the side of the *Titanic* the sailors saw the popular Purser standing calmly on the topmost deck."

Need it be added that one who was so brave was also a true Catholic? He had received Holy Communion shortly before sailing, and his last message to his brother was, "Do not forget me in your daily Mass."

Mr. McElroy had married in July, 1910, a daughter of Mr. John Ennis, J.P., of Ballymitty, Co. Wexford, formerly the well-known passenger Manager of the Allan Line. By a strange coincidence an old Cottonian, Mr. Octavio Biet, becoming acquainted with Mr. McElroy whilst they were both staying at the same hotel in Southampton just before the *Titanic* sailed, went to see him off. Neither knew that they both belonged to the same school. R.I.P.

* * *

We would also beg to express our condolence with Mr. Harold J. Ashcroft ('99) in his brother's death in the same terrible catastrophe.

We have also regretfully to record the death of Mr. Edward Pyke, J.P., of Southport (Sedgley Park, 1845). He died October 10th, 1911, at the age of 77. R.I.P.

* * *

We have received the following interesting notes from a correspondent in the Antipodes:—

Probably what I am about to write will to most of your readers appear very much like ancient history, for it has reference to two Parkers who left more than seventy years ago.

Mr. Archibald was master of the last " study " when I was put under him in October, 1840, and left at the Christmas following. I remember him as a young man and recollect that he appeared to employ some of his time in practising shorthand. From the time he left I never could ascertain what had become of him. Even Mr. Vinn, who loved to keep himself acquainted with the after history of boys who had been at the Park, could give me no information about him.

Not till 1866 did I learn that he was still amongst the living. On the feast of the Epiphany I received a letter from him with reference to two sons whom he wished to place in my care. He did not accept my terms and I again lost sight of him.

In 1888, about the middle of August, I was visiting Warrnambool (Australia), and the local newspaper published the fact. On the day that the paper appeared I spent some hours in travelling round the neighbourhood with a gentleman whom I had accompanied from New Zealand, and when our conveyance returned to our hotel a tall military-looking gentleman stepped up and asked my friend if he was Mr. Plunket. My friend, of course, referred him to me, with the result that the military-looking gentleman introduced himself and said his name was Archibald. I was delighted to see him, and found him a most interesting companion during the short time I was able to enjoy his society.

THE COTTONIAN.

He was custodian of the museum and, though it was after hours, he put himself to much trouble in describing the various exhibits.

I learned from him that he had come to Australia and had joined the police in Victoria in the early times. He had risen to the rank of Inspector and had recently retired on a pension. I have not seen him since and presume that he is dead. One of his sons founded a weekly newspaper called *The Bulletin*, which is probably the most popular journal in New South Wales.

The other old Parker I wish to refer to now is the Rev. Father Driscoll. He was sacristan at the Park when first I knew him, and I remember his putting on me a cassock and surplice when I was to take part in the procession on the feast of the Purification. He left in 1841, I think early in the year, and went to Old Hall, where he was ordained. It was not till 1865 that I again saw him. On the feast of the Epiphany, in that year, I met him at St. Francis' Presbytery, Melbourne. We had much to say to each other and on the following day he visited me at my house. He was about to leave Australia for New Zealand. In conversation with me he remarked on the fact that I had been, a few years previously, to England and back to Melbourne, and asked me if I had not felt nervous on the voyage. I told him I had not. He said that he was always extremely nervous when at sea. What he said then was greatly impressed upon my mind when, some little time later, I learned that the *City of Dunedin*, the steamer in which he was travelling round the west coast of the South Island, had been wrecked and all on board had perished. R.I.P. Not a single body was ever recovered.

* * *

Philip O. Bourlay ('76—'80) and his little daughter have both recently undergone a series of wonderfully successful operations in the Royal Southern Hospital, Liverpool. The trouble in each case was an obscure form of "infantile paralysis," which takes years to develope and gradually cripples the sufferer and about which many doctors know nothing. For the past twelve years Mr. Bourlay has been head of a printing business in Cardiff.

* * *

Walter Tarte (1874), now in Brisbane, Queensland, sends greetings to all 'Parkers' who may read and remember.

* * *

Tom Moore ('74) of Kandy, Ceylon, has received the *Cottonian* from his nephew Frank Moore ('91—'94), and desires his warmest remembrances to be conveyed to the next 'Old Boys' Meeting.' He hopes to be in England again soon and to revisit St. Wilfrid's.

* * *

Congratulations to Rev. J. Little and Rev. A. Bermingham, who received the diaconate in the English College, Lisbon, on March 23rd at the hands of Don Antonio Alves Ferreira, Bishop of Viseu.

* * *

Besides the large number of Old Boys who attended the annual meeting at Whitsuntide we have been pleased to welcome the following at different times during the term :—Charles J. Howell ('05), Octavio Biet ('03), Francis Roberts ('87), Adair Thompson ('11), Vincent Arnold ('12), and C Raymond Campbell ('07).

* * *

His many friends will be glad to hear that Peter T. Coolican (1900) who has recently been married, is head of one of the 17 postal districts into which Canada is divided. He is stationed at headquarters in the capital, Ottawa.

* * *

With deep regret we have to record the death of Bernard Joseph Dutton ('93), former District Judge of Matara, Ceylon. He relinquished his position and returned to England in May of last year, and died at his residence, Holway House, Holywell, on April 21st last, at the early age of 36 years. Mr. Dutton was a

St. Wilfrid's College

Is the direct successor of Sedgley Park School (1763-1873), the Training School of so many eminent Catholic Bishops and Clergy, as well as of a number of distinguished Catholic Laymen.

Situated above 800 feet above sea-level, and protected from the east and north-east by the Weaver Hills (1,500 feet).

A Course of PHYSICAL DRILL is taught according to the Modern

"Clease" System.

The Exercises have been specially chosen and supervised by Mr. F. MEREDITH CLEASE, formerly Director of Physical Exercises to the Birmingham Athletic Institute and the Birmingham Athletic Club, and now of the Clease Institute, New Bond Street, W.

The Course of Studies is both Classical & Commercial

The ANNUAL EXAMINATIONS held at the College enable Students to qualify for registration by :—

The General Medical Council.
Pharmaceutical Society of Great Britain.
Royal College of Veterinary Surgeons.
The Law Society.
The Institute of Civil Engineers.
The Institute of Chartered Accountants.

The Royal Institute of British Architects.
The Surveyors' Institution.
The Auctioneers' Institute.
The Institute of Actuaries.
The Institute of Chemistry.

OAKAMOOR STATION is on the Manchester to Burton Line (North Staffordshire Railway). From London and the South it may be reached via Stafford, Burton or Uttoxeter.

THE RECTOR, CANON HYMERS, will readily forward further information.

Chapter 10

The Canons Regular of the Lateran

St. Mary's Priory, Bodmin

St. Mary's Abbey,and Church Bodmin

Interior of St. Mary's Church Bodmn

The daily timetable for the canons in 1887 was as follows:

5.00am	Rise
5.30am	Meditation
6.30am	Prime & Tierce
6.45am	Conventual Mass
7.30am	Breakfast
7.45am	Chant & Liturgy
9.00am	Lectures
12.30pm	Sext, Nones & Examen
1.00pm	Dinner
1.30pm	Recreation
2.15pm	Silence
2.30pm	Vespers & Compline
3.00pm	Study
3.30pm	Classes
4.30pm	Recreation
5.00pm	Study
7.30pm	Supper
8.00pm	Recreation
8.30pm	Matins & Laudes
9.15pm	Examination of conscience
9.30pm	Retire

Education of the Canons

The alumnate (or juniorate) was a school for boys who showed signs of a vocation to the Order. This was always small and as an educational institution it was more a private tutoring establishment than a school. One of the tasks was to learn sufficient Latin for further study towards the priesthood. The first alumnate was established at Marnhull in Dorset in 1888 – this was an establishment of about 20 boys. In 1891 the alumnate was moved to Bodmin Priory in Cornwall and in 1907 back to Swanage in Dorset where a large house had been built for this purpose. After a few years the Canons were offered a church and parish at Eton by the Bishop of Northampton. Since there was also a large house suitable for a few boys the nearness of London persuaded the Superior of the time to make another move to Eton. Eton, however, was not really suitable and in 1923 a house was built at Datchet surrounded by six or seven acres of ground. This closed in 1968 due to the increasing standards required for all schools.

At the age of 16 upwards a boy entered the Novitiate. In 1884 the Novitiate was at Bodmin but in 1891 it was transferred to Spettisbury for three years after which it went back to Bodmin where it remained until 1976. The young men in the Novitiate spent at least a year in the Novitiate after which they took Simple Vows. Solemn Vows were usually taken three years after this.

Studies for the priesthood took six years. These were done at the House of Studies or Professorium. St. Monica's at Spettisbury was the Professorium between 1887 and 1907. Some of the very academically able young men were sent away to the International College in Rome for two or three years for further studies.

Lay brothers were concerned solely with manual labour and with the secular affairs of the Community. They were mostly pious men, who while unable to attain to the degree of learning requisite for Holy Orders, were yet drawn to the religious life and able by their toil to contribute to the prosperity of the order.

Abbot Menchini, the Visitor, made a canonical visitation of St. Monica's and together with White, the Prior of Marnhull and Fr. John Higgins, interviewed the eleven members in simple vows: these were in retreat to assess their situation and to decide whether or not they had a religious vocation. Four of the young men were dismissed as they were "lacking spirit and motive and so not called to religious life." One had his solemn profession delayed for a year and was sent to Bodmin, but Isodor O'Leary made his solemn profession on 23rd October and was then sent for higher studies at the International College in Rome.

In November there seemed to have been some disciplinary problems at the priory. Two of the students, who had been allowed to go home for a time as an experiment, were found guilty of "serious infringement against regular discipline." In consequence, the Visitor ordered that they should be sent home again. Others guilty of less serious offences were subjected to 30 days of penance. Both the offenders were back at St. Monica's by 20th February 1891.

November must have been a very disheartening time for Prior Allaria. Another of his students, Norbert Jones, was ordered to Bodmin to replace Thomas Belton who had been "called to Rome to perfect himself in study and religious discipline" and so from a total of 14 students in May, there were now only four.

In May and June of 1891 there was an Extraordinary Visitation by Abbott Alphonsus Lalli, Visitor of the Roman Province with his socius Fr. Archangelo Lolli. Abbott Lalli was not fond of English weather. He had an abiding memory of "almost continual rain." "Oh! the winter in England is horrible . . . longe, longe a me." Nor was he enamoured of the Priory cuisine. "Meals are always without wine, no soup or milk, just a bit of half-cooked meat and a glass of beer, that is all." During the two months, they carried out a very thorough inspection of the place and personnel of St. Monica's, Spettisbury, St.Joseph's, Marnhull and St. Mary's, Bodmin. It was decided that Marnhull should be given up and sold, with the Juniorate being transferred to Bodmin, and that the Novitiate should be transferred from Bodmin to Spettisbury. Allaria was now not only Prior of Spettisbury but also made 'quasi' Visitor of the Province of England in the absence of a Visitor. (Menchini had been recalled to Rome) Higgins was to be Master of the Professed and parish priest for Spettisbury with Honiton and Laird was to be Master of Novices and Procurator.

Cuthbert McAdam, a student transferred from Bodmin to Spettisbury, was appointed infirmarian and suggested that the room above the library used as the infirmary should be "rendered more lightsome by the provision of more fenestration."

In June 1894 Belton (who had been in Australia for three years for health reasons) came to Spettisbury to discuss the setting up of a London Mission. This had been agreed with Cardinal Vaughan and was eventually established at Stroud Green. It meant a lot of changes for St. Monica's. That autumn Higgins left Spettisbury for Stroud Green, Aloyius Smith left to go to Rome for higher studies, McAdam left to go to Bodmin as Procurator and O'Connor left with all the novices to go to Bodmin as Novice master. On the other hand, Jones returned from Bodmin and Hannigan and Holden returned from Rome (Hannigan as the new master of the Professed)

In October 1897 there was a crisis meeting in Spettisbury to discuss "the debts under which is house laboured" O'Connor and McAdam arrived from Bodmin and White from London. They discussed closing down Bodmin and selling the land and moving the Novitiate back to Spettisbury among other options. There seems to have been some disagreements. McAdam wrote "If you keep this place (Spettisbury) it will cost £250 a year at least, for it will soon want new roofing and is ever in repair." In the event the Novitiate was not transferred although McAdam was: he took over the office of master of the professed from Isodore O'Leary.

In the autumn of 1898 the Spettisbury 'Schola' sang at the requiem for Canon Debbaudt in Canon Wymouth and for Twohey in Axminster: they also sang at the opening of Canon Scoles Church in Tisbury. In December they sang at the Requiem for Mgr. John Grainger in Exmouth: he was a generous benefactor—his bequests to Bodmin, Spettisbury and Stroud Green "rescued the former two from their crippling debts."

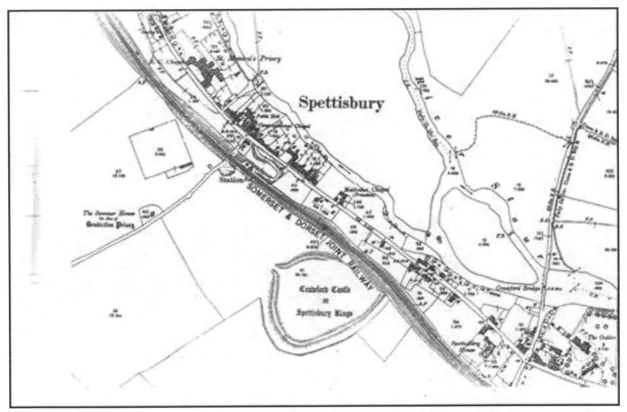

Map of the village of Spettisbury, showing St. Monica's Priory

St. Monica's Priory showing the Chapel to the left

St. Monica's Priory showing the Priests' House (Village Hall)
and other buildings to the right

One of the last pictures taken at St. Monica's Priory, Spettisbury in 1907

Front Row (left to right) Joseph O'Connor, Cuthbert McAdam (Prior), Bernard Cotter
Back Row (centre) Bro. Anthony Fitzgerald

In the census taken on 5th April 1891 at St. Monica's Priory had a Community of two Priests, two lay workers and seven students training to be priests.

The Priory, Main Road (11M)

Name	Occupation		Age	Place of Birth
Anthony Allaria	RC Priest		38	Italy
Gilbert Higgins	RC Priest (Prefect of Discipline)		41	Ireland
Leo Holden	Theological Student		21	Clitheroe, Lancs
Charles Hannigan	Theological Student		20	Portland, Dorset
Joseph O'Connor	Theological Student		21	Ireland
Gaudentius Holden	Theological Student		18	Longbridge, Lancs
Aloysius Smith	Theological Student		14	Weymouth, Dorset
Stephen Lyons	Theological Student		21	London
Raymond Carroll	Theological Student		18	Newport, Isle of Wight
Robert McGrath	Lay Worker in Monastery	(deaf)	39	Preston, Lancs
Joseph Corr	Lay Worker in Monastery		24	Axminster, Devon

Ten years later in the 1901 census St. Monica's Community had 8 priests, 4 lay brothers and 7 students. Priory House was part of the main property but may have been let to tenants. (Prior Anthony Allaria must have been absent on the day of the census).

The Priory (19M)

Name	Occupation	Age	Place of Birth
Isidore O'Leary	Roman Catholic Priest	30	Exeter, Devon
Wilfred Regan	Roman Catholic Priest	26	Devonport, Devon
Cuthbert McAdam	Roman Catholic Priest	43	Hereford
Phillip Corr	Roman Catholic Priest	27	Chardstock, Devon
Edward Bovenizer	Roman Catholic Priest	26	Plymouth, Devon
Thomas Mullins	Roman Catholic Priest	25	Donhead, Wilts
Vincent Scully	Roman Catholic Priest	24	Lambeth, Surrey
Michael Reddin	Roman Catholic Priest	29	Ireland
Francis Jeffrey	Theological Student	26	Salisbury, Wilts
Clement McGuiness	Theological Student	22	Liverpool, Lancs
Charles Brighton	Theological Student	21	Birmingham, Warwicks
Bernard Cotter	Theological Student	26	Ireland
Ambrose Mellish	Theological Student	34	Reigate, Surrey
Joseph O'Reilly	Theological Student	15	Birkenhead, Cheshire
Matthew Gallacher	Theological Student	16	Scotland
Austin Clayton	Lay Brother	34	London
Arthur Pearce	Lay Brother	22	Sherborne, Dorset
Owen Kelly	Lay Brother	15	Liverpool, Lancs
William Bishop	Boarder	35	London

Priory House

James Mcloughlan	Retired Indian Service	59	Ireland
Jane? Mcloughlan	Wife	49	York
Norah Fitzgibbon	Domestic houseservant	19	Ireland

1901 An indication of the state of the house is given in May when Fr. Philip Corr was leaving for Bodmin. "The brethren bid dieu to Fr. Corr, A large portion of the ceiling at the main entrance fell down just as Bro. Thomas Mullins was passing."

In 1902 Cuthbert McAdam took over from Anthony Allaria as Prior of St. Monica's. He was the very antithesis of his predecessor, an engaging personality and a genial conversationalist; he invited confidence and had an easy rapport with the young. He had wide interests, varied acquaintances and practical concerns. He brought "a little alleviation to the primitive austerities" of the house. He took advice about the possibility of introducing electricity into the house and church and introduced the "oil engine from Charlton Barrow" onto the premises and got it working the pump at 2.30 pm on 4th January. Whether this was to pump drinking water into the tanks or the floodwater with its "pestiferous odour" into the river, is not known.

Canons associated with St. Monica's Priory, Spettisbury & St.Joseph's Priory, Marnhull, Dorset and also St. Mary's, Bodmin Priory, Cornwall.

Abbot Felix Menchini

Felix Menchini was sent to England in 1881 to restore the order. He was Prior of Bodmin and Visitor of the English Province from 1884 to 1891 when he was recalled to Rome. He was involved in the negotiations for Marnhull and Spettisbury and visited both many times. He acted as a trouble-shooter on many occasions.

Abbot Felix Menchini

Cuthbert McAdam

Cuthbert McAdam, born Henry Martyn Eccles McAdam on 17th September 1857 in Hereford, was the third Prior of Spettisbury (1902-1907). In 1891 he arrived at Spettisbury from Bodmin in simple vows and was made infirmarian. In 1894 he returned to Bodmin as Procurator and in 1897 was the Catholic Chaplain to Her Majesty's Prison. He returned to Spettisbury in 1898 as Master of the Professed. In 1907 he took the community to Swanage where he died in 1916.

Augustine White

Augustine White, born about 1858 in Hammersmith as Henry St. George White, studied at Prior Park College, near Bath and was ordained in 1884. He arrived from Bodmin in 1884 to become Prior of Marnhull. When Marnhull was closed he returned to Cornwall as Prior of Bodmin (1891-1894). He then went to London to look after the Mission at Stroud Green. He died in 1932; a memorial at Christchurch Priory says "this plaque is also in memory of the Rev. Augustine White, Titular Abbot of Holy Cross Abbey, Waltham and leader of the Canons Regular of the Lateran."

Joseph O'Connor

Joseph O'Connor was born about 1870 in Dublin, Ireland. In 1887 he arrived at Spettisbury from Bodmin in simple vows. He was ordained in 1891 and in 1893 made master of Novices at Spettisbury. He also shared the Ministry of Honiton with Cleary. In 1894 he went to Bodmin as Master of Novices and in 1896 was made Prior of Bodmin. He returned to Spettisbury in 1900 and was still there in 1907.

Wilfred Regan

Wilfred Regan was born about 1875 in Devonport, Devon as William Regan. In 1890 he was in the alumnate at Marnhull and he came to Spettisbury in 1891 making his profession two years later. In 1896 he was sent to Shap Cell to help in the school for boys but was back in Spettisbury in 1898. In 1899 he was made Master of the Professed and in 1901 was sent to Bodmin.

Michael Reddin

Michael Redden was born about 1872 in Ireland. He was at Spettisbury in 1894 but then went to Bodmin for two years returning in 1899. In 1901 he was sent to Bodmin again and in 1902 said the first mass at St. Ives.

Aloysius Smith

Aloysius Smith was born about 1874 in Weymouth, Dorset as Walter James Smith. He was a pupil at Marnhull in 1884 and in 1887 went to Bodmin for his novitiate. He arrived at Spettisbury in 1890 and made his solemn profession in 1893. In 1894 he went to Rome for higher studies until 1900 when he returned to Bodmin where he was made Superior. In 1902 he was made Prior of Bodmin and in 1905 Visitor of the English Province. In 1946 he was elected Abbot General, the first Englishman in the 500 year history of the order. In 1952 he was enthroned as Abbot of Bodmin. He died on 20th Aug 1960 at Hayle and was buried at Bodmin.

Aloysius Smith

Philip Corr

Philip Corr was born about 1874 in Chardstock, Devon. He attended Marnhull Juniorate but left in 1890 for the Novitiate at Bodmin. In 1891 he went to Spettisbury where he made his solemn profession in 1893. In 1902 he was transferred to Bodmin and in 1908 was at Stroud Green.

Edward Bovenizer

Edward Bovenizer was born about 1874 in Plymouth, Devon as Peter Joseph Bovenizer. He attended Marnhull Juniorate but left in 1891 for the Novitiate at Bodmin. He went to Spettisbury in 1893, made his solemn profession in 1898 and was ordained in 1889. He remained at Spettisbury for some years. In 1908 he was at Stroud Green.

Bruno Peters

Bruno Peters was in Bodmin in 1894 as a novice and arrived in Spettisbury in 1896 where he remained until sent to Bodmin in 1901 as Master of Novices.

Francis Jeffrey

Francis Jeffrey was born about 1875 in Salisbury, Wilts as John Jeffrey. He was a student at Spettisbury from about 1892 both as a novice and in vows. He remained at Spettisbury at least until 1903.

Basil Landreth

Basil Landreth was born 16th Oct 1875 in Southport, Lancs. to a non-catholic family who all converted. He entered Marnhull in 1890 and in 1903 took simple vows. In 1904 he completed his novitiate and went from Bodmin to Spettisbury. That same year he had a heart problem and at the end of July caught typhoid fever. He died on 30th Sep 1904 aged 28 and was buried in the cemetery at Spettisbury

Raymund Gallagher

Raymund Gallagher completed his novitiate at Bodmin in 1903 and then entered Spettisbury as a student.

Riley

Riley completed his novitiate at Bodmin in 1903 and then entered Spettisbury as a student.

R. A. Vaughan

R. A. Vaughan was a convert Anglican Minister who in 1903 was accepted as novice. He completed his novitiate and went from Bodmin to Spettisbury to do Philosophy.

Alphonsus McElroy

Alphonsus McElroy was born about 1878 in Liverpool, Lancs. as Richard McElroy. In 1890 he was a pupil at Marnhull and after his novitiate at Bodmin, arrived at Spettisbury in 1904. In 1911 he was made Prior of Bodmin, a post he held for many years. In 1942 he entered hospital for a slight operation but died 4 days later and was buried at Bodmin.

Those who did not persevere"

John Cleary

John Cleary, a former Marnhull boy, arrived at Spettisbury in 1887 and stayed until 1890 when Menchini suggested he leave.

Alipius Hughes

Alipius Hughes, a former Marnhull boy, arrived at Spettisbury in 1887. He returned to Bodmin in 1889 for a while to establish his religious vocation but in 1890 Menchini suggested he leave.

Maurice Suckling

Maurice Suckling, born about 1871 in London, arrived at Marnhull in 1886. He came to Spettisbury in 1887 and stayed until 1890 when Menchini suggested he leave.

Edgar Sheldon

Edgar Sheldon, a former Marnhull boy, arrived at Spettisbury in 1887 and stayed until 1890 when Menchini suggested he leave.

Richard O'Regan

Richard O'Regan, a former Marnhull boy, went to Bodmin in 1887 and to Spettisbury in 1888. In 1890 his simple vows were dispensed on account of his ill health which rendered him unsuitable for religious life.

Hugh McElroy

Hugh McElroy, born about 1875 in Liverpool, attended Marnhull Juniorate and in 1890 went to Bodmin for his novitiate. In 1891 he arrived at Spettisbury where on the order of the Abbot General his simple vows were dispensed, on account of doubt on religious vocation and Hugh left in 1892. He became a purser and in 1912 went down with the Titanic. Hugh sent two postcards from the Royal Southampton Yacht Club before the Titanic left. One to Phillip Corr dated 6th April 1912 read as follows: "Many thanks for your letter and good wishes which I reciprocate, the Titanic is in many ways an improved Olympic and will I trust be a success, I am sorry I could not get down to Swanage this time but I was tied to Southampton and the train service too erratic to take chances, all kind of messages to you both." The other card was to Cuthbert McAdam at Bodmin Priory; this was also dated 6th April 1912 with a message in a similar vein.

William Carroll

William Carroll, born about 1873 in Newport, Isle of Wight as Raymond Carroll, was a former Marnhull boy who went to Bodmin in 1887 and to Spettisbury in 1888. He remained until 1891 when he received dispensation from his simple vows.

John O'Connell

John O'Connell, a former Marnhull boy, went to Bodmin in 1887 and to Spettisbury in 1888. In 1890 he was banished home for several months for serious infringements of discipline. He later received dispensation from his simple vows and had gone by the end of 1891.

Stephen Lyons

Stephen Lyons, born about 1870 in London a former Marnhull boy, went to Bodmin in 1887 and to Spettisbury in 1888. In 1890 he was banished home for several months for serious infringements of discipline. He later received dispensation from his simple vows and had gone by the end of 1891.

Spettisbury Station 1910

St. Monica's Priory

About 1894 Back row (left to right) Sebastian Rota, unknown, Philip Corr, Gaudentius Holden, Wifred Regan, Laurence Donelan, Vincent Scully
Front row Thomas Mullins, Norbert Jones, Prior Anthony Allaria, Leo Holden, Edward Bovenizer

Abbot Felix Menchini also arrived and gave Tonsure & Minor orders to Francis Jeffrey, McGuiness, Brighton & Cotter after which he went to Bodmin to deal with the business of the house and to settle the differences which had arisen among the brethren. He remained in Bodmin until August the following year.

Back row: (left to right) Francis Jeffrey, Thomas Mullins, McGuiness, unknown, Brighton, unknown, Edward Bovenizer, Philip Corr
Middle row: unknown, Sellon, unknown, Bruno Peters, Michael Reddin, Cotter, Bro. Clayton, McGregor, Vincent Scully
Front row: McAdam, O'Leary, Prior Anthony Allaria, Wilfred Regan, O'Connor, Hannigan

In August, Bishop Graham came for the ordinations of Reddin and Peters as deacons and Bovenizer, Mullins and Scully as priests (the last of the Marnhull alumni).

Back row (left to right) Regan, Bovenizer, unknown, Cotter, unknown, Mullins, unknown, Scully, unknown
Middle row McAdam, unknown, McGuiness, Sellon, unknown, Brighton, Hannigan
Front row unknown, Bruno Peters, Prior Anthony Allaria, Bishop Graham, Michael Reddin, Francis Jeffrey, unknown

In September 1895 Bishop Graham came to St. Monica's for the ordinations of Holden, Donelan and Corr as sub-deacons.

Back row (left to right) Gaudentius Holden, Laurence Donelan, C.P. (Passionist)
Front Row (left to right) C.P. Bishop Graham, Philip Corr

On 29th September 1896 Bishop Graham came to St. Monica's to celebrate an Ordination Mass which was "solemnly sung by the rest of the community." George McGregor and Wilfrid Regan were made sub-deacons and Gaudentius Holden and Philip Corr, deacons.

Back Row (left to right) Wilfred Regan, George McGregor
Front Row (left to right) Philip Corr, Bishop Graham, Gaudentius Holden

Among the 15 members of the 'gentry' living in Spettisbury who were noted in the Kelly's Directory of 1903 were seven members of the community of St. Monica's.

Rev Anthony Allaria D.D. (visitor)	The Priory
Rev Edward Bovenizer	The Priory
Rev Francis Jeffry	The Priory
Very Rev Cuthbert McAdam (prior)	The Priory
Rev Geo McGregor D.D.	The Priory
Rev Joseph O'Connor	The Priory
Rev Vincent Scully	The Priory

*The Novitiate in 1903. William Riley.
Richard McElroy. Basil Landreth.
Bruno Peters, CRL. Novice Master.*

The celebration of Bodmin's Golden Jubilee. Photo taken at the Canonesses' Priory of St. Augustine, Abbotskerswell. Bishop Barrett is seated between Ab. A. White and Fr. G. Higgins, the first members of the English Province. On extreme left of the Bishop Prior McElroy and on extreme right Fr. W. Fox, chaplain. 23.6.1931.

St. Monica's Priory. **(today)**

I moved with my husband into Priory Cottage, No. 1 St. Monica's Priory in 2002 and have been fascinated with the history of the place ever since. This website is the result of my research. If you have any comments, corrections or any further information about the Priory, please email me.
Sue Stead
<u>sue@Spettisbury.c</u>

St Peter in Chains, Stroud Green in London
Womersley Road, Tottenham, Greater London N8 9

Holy Ghost and St. Edward the King and Martyr, Swanage.

Church Name changed to
The Church of the Holy Spirit and St Edwards, Victoria Avenue, Swanage.
Father T. Dolan, The Presbytery, 1 Victoria Avenue, Swanage Tel: 01929/422491
To the left of the church was the The Alumnate, which is now the home of the Parish Priest

Chapter 11

Special Acknowledgments and References

Special Thanks for all your help and contributions

Veronica Jones (UK) the Daughter of Hugh McElroy's godson, who has been invaluable in checking my work and writing the Forward of this biology of Great Uncle Hugh.

also to John Hilton (Bodmin UK) for all your help in collating Canons Regular of the Lateran material, and for being a true friend.

Inger Sheil (AUS) a person I have come to admire very much, for her determination in fact finding, also for her help in discovering the true subject names in some photos, especially those from the R.M.S. Olympic.

Rev Gerald O'Leary CC (St Peters Church, Ballymitty) (IRE)
John & Patience Nolan, "Springwood" Tullycanna, Ballymitty in Wexford, Also Edna.
Brian Ticehurst (Researcher, Southampton) (UK)
Ernie Luck (UK)
John Hemmert (USA)
Jackie McElroy (USA)
Mr G. Meanwell (France). (Extract)
Teri Milch (USA)
Alfred Grech (Malta) (Grandson of Mr Octavio Biet)

Special Acknowledgments

Sheila Jemima of the Southampton Oral History Archives (Extract/Photo)
Sara Smyth and Bróna Olwill of the National Library of Ireland in Dublin. (Photo)
Mrs Marianne Hulland, Head of Communications, St Edmundsbury Borough Council. (Extract)
Mrs Grace Cory, Bodmin Town Council, Mrs Janet Wright, Bodmin library,
Mrs Tooze, Bodmin Town Museum. (Extract/Photo)
Dave Wilson & Jos Trinham; The Cottonian Archives, Cotton Hall (Extract/ Photo's also copy of the "The Cottonian" St Wilfrins College (Newsletter Vol 2—No1) Midsummer 1912.
Dr Amanda Beven & Sister Barbara, St Joseph Archivist, Birmingham Archdiocesan Archives, C/o St Joseph Convent, Gosford Green, Coventry (Extract)
Mrs. Cassebeer Accounts, Courtesy of Michael Poirier from the Mike Poirier Collection (Article)
Senan Molony, (Extract)
Jo Rodriquez (Extract) James Kearne, SS Cedric (Grandfather)
Encyclopedia Titanica (Drawing)
Park Lane Posters (Poster)
D.K. (Photo)
The Canadian Pacific Railway (Photo)
Father Farancis Brown Collection (Photo)
Titanic Concepts (Steve Santin's) (Photo)
Sue Stead, The History of St. Monica's Priory, Spettisbury, Dorset

Special References

US Senate Inquiry
British Inquiry (Wreck Commissioners" Court)
Public Record Office, "R.M.S. Titanic: The True Story" Kew, 1999 (CD-ROM.)
Probate Records (London 31st July 1912)
Mansion House R.M.S. Titanic Relief Fund Booklets and Minute Books March 1913
The Minute Book of the Southampton Committee of the R.M.S. Titanic Relief Fund, November 1914
Documents Agg & Acc (PRO London BT100/259)
English Census 1871, 1881, 1891, 1901 (Liverpool) and 1891 (Bodmin) 1891 (Leicester, Staffs)
Irish Census 1911 (Wexford)
Public Archives of Nova Scotia (Photo's)
Adrian Jobson, Remote Enquiries Service Manager, the National Archives, Kew. (Extracts/Photo's)

Book References

Violet Jessop and her book "R.M.S. Titanic, Survivor, the memoirs of Violet Jessop". (Extracts)
Father Eddie O'Donnell "Father Browne's R.M.S. Titanic". (Extracts/Photo's)
Walter Lord (1976) "A Night to Remember". (Extracts)
Sir Bertram Hayes, K.C.M.G., D.S.O. "Hull Down", Master of the Majestic". (Extracts)
Fr.Ambrose Whitehead, "100 Years in Cornwall. The History of a Canon Regular Ministry".
A Fanning, "A Titanic Story", (Priory & Abbey, Bodmin)
"The City of Coventry: Roman catholicism", A History of the County of Warwick: Volume 8: The City of Coventry and Borough of Warwick (1969), pp. 368-371. URL: http://www.british-history.ac.uk/report.aspx?compid= 16040 Date accessed: 09 January 1994.

Newspaper References

Mike Thomson, Newspaper Heritage Microfilm and Newspaper Archive of America,
The New York Times (Articles/Extracts/Photo)
The Washington Post (Extracts/Photo)
The Evening Telegram (Extracts/Photo)
Colorado Springs Gazette (Extracts/Photo)
The Evening Independent (Extracts/Photo)
The Fort Wayne Sentinel (Extracts/Photo)
The Anoconda Standard (Extracts/Photo)
The Cork Examiner (County Cork, Ireland) 12th April 1912 (Extracts/Photo)
The Western Morning News, 19th April 1912 (Article)
The Atlantic Daily Bulletin, 24th April 1999 [Brian Ticehurst] (Article)
The West Briton and Cornwall Advertiser, 25th April 1912 (Article)
Josh Birchall, The Coventry Standard, 27th April 1912 (Article)
Cornish Guardian, 30th April 1998 (Extracts)
The Shipping Times (Extracts)